Visual Reference Basics

Microsoft®
Word 97

Maria Reidelbach

Acknowledgements

Project Manager
Marni Ayers

English Editors
Marni Ayers
Aegina Berg

Technical Editor
Aegina Berg

Layout and Design
Jeffrey A. Bates
Shawn Morningstar

First DDC Publishing, Inc. Printing

10   9   8   7   6   5   4   3   2   1

Printed in the United States of America.

Table of Contents

BASIC SKILLS

FORMAT CHARACTERS

FORMAT PAGES

EDITING INFORMATION

TABLES

GRAPHICS

ADVANCED TOOLS

Index

Introduction

DDC's Visual Reference Basics series is designed to help you make the most of your Microsoft software. Newly updated to reflect changes and enhancements in Microsoft 97 applications, the Visual Reference Basics are equally useful as instruction manuals or as desktop reference guides for the experienced user. With illustrations and clear explanations of every step involved, they make even complex processes easy to understand and follow.

The most distinctive feature of this series is its extensive use of visuals. Buttons, toolbars, screens and commands are all illustrated so that there is never any doubt that you are performing the right actions. Most information can be understood at a glance, without a lot of reading through dense and complicated instructions. With Visual Reference Basics, you learn what you need to know quickly and easily.

This book contains one hundred functions essential for optimal use of Word. These functions are logically sequenced and arranged for ease of use. Basic skills are the first covered, with more advanced functions building on the skills that were previously taught. Cross-references in chapters help you to find related topics. Notes on each page give additional information or tips to supplement the directions given. The only thing you need to get the most out of the Visual Reference Basics series is a basic understanding of Windows and the desire to become more familiar with Word.

The Visual Reference Basics series is an informative and convenient way to acquaint yourself with the capabilities of your Microsoft application. It is a valuable resource for anyone who wants to become a power user of Microsoft 97 software.

Basic Skills

This section will give you the basic tools of file management. You will learn how to create a new document and open a previously saved document; how to view, move through, save and close a document. You will learn how to set options and customize your screen, as well as how to get help within Word. You will also be able to print documents, envelopes and labels.

Arrange Windows

You can open several documents at once and layer or tile them. You can also open two windows within a document or split a document window and view two separate parts at once.

Window ➡️ **Type Number of Document**

Notes:

- To show all windows on the desktop, right-click the taskbar background and click Tile Horizontally or Tile Vertically.

- Change the setting on the General tab of the Options dialog (see **Options**) to display your text in white on a blue background.

Bring a Window to the Front

Click on any visible part of the window.

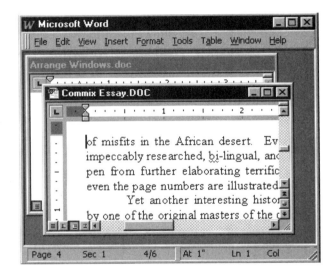

OR

1 Click **Window**.

2 Click desired document name at bottom part of menu, or press document number on the keyboard.

Notes:

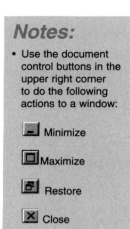

- Use the document control buttons in the upper right corner to do the following actions to a window:

  ▬ Minimize

  ▢ Maximize

  ▣ Restore

  ☒ Close

Tile Windows Horizontally

1 Click **W**indow, **A**rrange All.

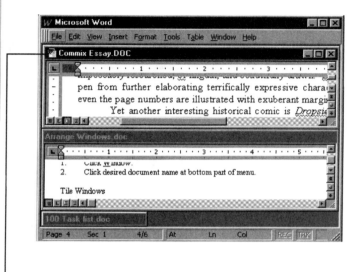

2 The title bar of the active document is displayed in the brighter color.

Arrange Windows *continued . . .*

You can open several documents at once and layer or tile them. You can also open two windows within a document or split a document window and view two separate parts at once.

Notes:

- Splitting windows enables you to view two separate sections of a document simultaneously. For example, you may need to compare information in the first paragraph of a long report with information in the last paragraph. Splitting the document window enables you to view both sections onscreen at the same time.

Split Document Window

1 Click and drag the **Split Box** down to the desired new location.

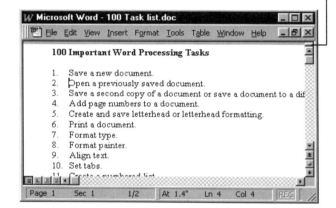

2 Each pane will have its own scroll buttons.

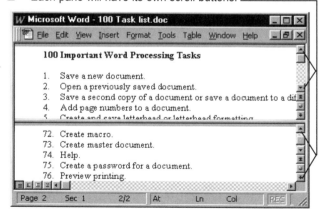

4

Open Another Window on a Document

1 Click **Window**, **New Window** to open another window within the same document.

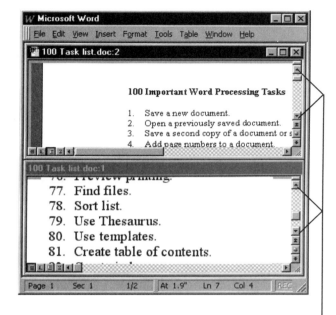

2 Each window will have its own scroll buttons, and the document can also be seen in different View types (see **View Document**). Editing to information in either window will be saved to the same file.

Envelopes

Use the envelope feature to quickly format, address, and print an envelope.

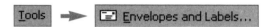

Notes:

- You can change the return address in the User Information tab of the Options dialog box (see **Options and Preferences**).

1 View letter (Word will automatically find the addressee)
OR
Select name and address to use on envelope, if desired.

2 Click **Tools**, **Envelopes and Labels** to open the Envelopes and Labels dialog box.

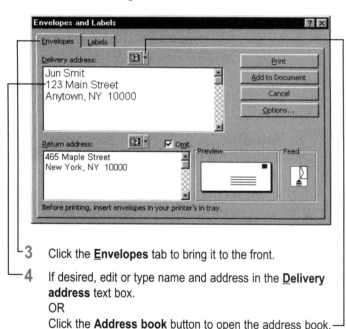

3 Click the **Envelopes** tab to bring it to the front.

4 If desired, edit or type name and address in the **Delivery address** text box.
OR
Click the **Address book** button to open the address book.

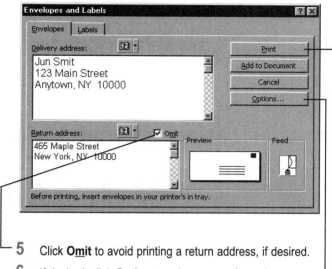

5   Click **O<u>m</u>it** to avoid printing a return address, if desired.

6   If desired, click **<u>O</u>ptions** to change envelope size, font type and size, or position of address.

7   Click **<u>P</u>rint** to send the envelope to the printer

OR

Click **<u>A</u>dd to Document** to add a page containing the envelope to the current document.

Folders and Files

Documents are stored in files, which are organized in folders. Whenever you open or save a document, you will be using folders and files.

1 Whether you choose to Open, do an initial Save, or Save As, a similar dialog box will open.

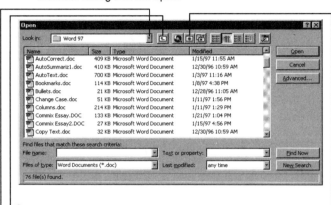

2 Choose the desired folder:

- Click the **Up One Level** button to display the folders stored along with the folder currently displayed in the Look in text box.
- Double-click a folder icon in the list window to display the contents of that folder.
- Click the **Look in Favorites** button to display favorite folders that you have chosen.
- Click the **Look in** drop-down button to choose another disk drive.

8

Notes:

- If a preview is taking too long to display, press Esc to cancel the preview.

3 Choose how the list box displays your files:

- Click the List button to show as many files as possible.
- Click the Details button to show file information, such as size, type and date modified.

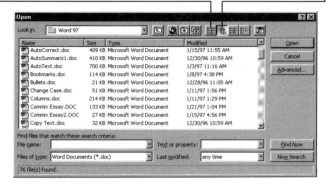

- Click the Properties button to show even more file information, including revision and printing history.
- Click the Preview button to display a thumbnail image of the file.

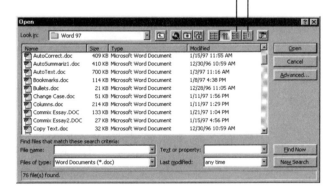

9

Folders and Files *continued . . .*

Documents are stored in files, which are organized in folders. Whenever you open or save a document, you will be using folders and files.

Notes:

- You can use an asterisk (∗) as a wild card in the Find File name field of the Open dialog box. The asterisk will stand for one or more characters.

- Click the Advanced button in the Open dialog box to save file search criteria.

Find File

Search in a number of folders at once for files similar to your description.

1 In the Open dialog box, display desired folder in the **Look in** text box.

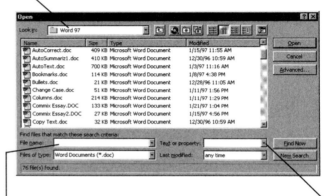

2 You may select any or all of the following options:
- In the **File name** text box, type the desired filename to search for, if desired.
- In the **Text or property** text box, type the text within file to search for, or file property, if desired.

10

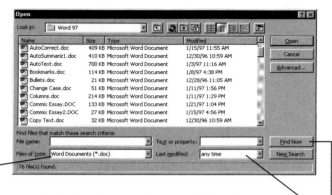

- In the **Files of type** text box, click the drop-down button and choose file type.
- In the **Last modified** text box, click the drop-down button and choose date range.

3 Click **Find Now**. The files matching your description will appear in the list box.

Help

Word's on-screen help gives you access to a wealth of detailed assistance and information.

Notes:

- The keyboard short-cut for accessing Help is F1.

- Add a bookmark to an important Help screen by clicking the Options button. (See **Options and Preferences**.)

Office Assistant

The office assistant provides context-sensitive help and allows you to type questions in plain English. (See **Office Assistant** for more info.)

1   On the Standard toolbar, click the Office Assistant

button
OR
Click **Help, Microsoft Word Help**.

2   Type your question or click desired choice.

3   When finished, click **Cancel**.

What's This?

Use **What's This** to point at mysterious buttons, menu choices and screen objects. You can also point at text or objects onscreen to receive formatting information.

1   Click **Help, What's This?** The pointer becomes a question mark and pointer.

2   Point and click at anything onscreen.

3   When you are finished, click **Esc** to revert to a normal pointer
OR
Click **Help, What's This?** again.

Contents and Index Help

Access Word's help files directly for the most thorough listing of help topics.

1 Click **Help**, **Contents and Index** to open the Help dialog box.

2 Click a tab for the kind of help you need:
- **Contents** tab: most useful to methodically learn about Word's features. Follow the on-screen instructions.
- **Index** tab: most useful to find information about feature details. Follow the on-screen instructions.
- **Find** tab: when you can't find the information you need anywhere else. The entire text of the help database is searched for your key words.

3 When finished, click **Cancel**.

Highlight Text

Use the highlighter to make important text stand out.

1   On the Standard toolbar, click the **Highlight** button .

2   Click and drag over text to highlight.
    OR
    Click the **Highlight** button .
    Type text.

3   To return to normal text, click the **Highlight** button to turn it off.

Change Highlight Color.

1   Click the **Highlight** drop-down button .

2   Choose desired highlight color.

Continue

Labels

Use the labels feature to create and format a sheet of repeating labels or a single label.

Tools ➡ 🖼 Envelopes and Labels...

Notes:

- Custom labels can be defined by clicking the New Label button in the Label Options dialog box.

- To print a complete sheet of return address labels for yourself, type your own address once in the Envelopes and Labels dialog box and select the Full page of the Same label option.

1 View letter (Word will automatically find the addressee)

OR

Select name and address to use on labels, if desired.

2 Click **Tools**, **Envelopes and Labels** to open the Envelopes and Labels dialog box.

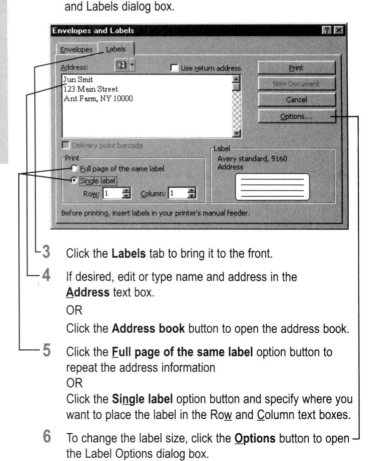

3 Click the **Labels** tab to bring it to the front.

4 If desired, edit or type name and address in the **Address** text box.

OR

Click the **Address book** button to open the address book.

5 Click the **Full page of the same label** option button to repeat the address information

OR

Click the **Single label** option button and specify where you want to place the label in the Row and Column text boxes.

6 To change the label size, click the **Options** button to open the Label Options dialog box.

- Word has the ability to print labels to pre-formatted label sheets according to product number. For example, if you purchase a package of labels, most likely Word will be able to match the product number in the Label Options dialog box. If not, you can customize a sheet of labels to suit your printing needs (by clicking the Options button).

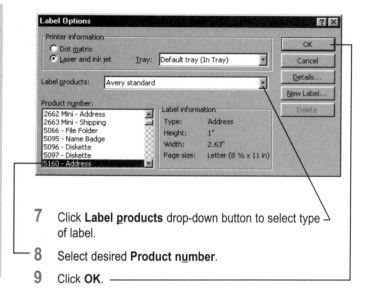

7 Click **Label products** drop-down button to select type of label.

8 Select desired **Product number**.

9 Click **OK**.

10 Click **Print** to send the labels to the printer.
OR
Click **New Document** to create new labels.

Mistakes: How to Undo

Everyone makes mistakes! Luckily, in Word you can undo most of them.

1 When you realize you've made a mistake,

click **Edit**, **Undo Typing**,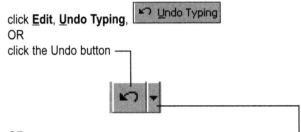
OR
click the Undo button

OR
To undo more than one step, click the **Undo drop-down** button, then click desired number of steps to undo.

2 To redo a step, click **Edit**, **Redo Typing**, or click the Redo button

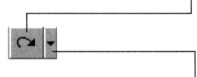

OR
To redo more than one step, click the **Redo drop-down** button, then click desired number of steps to redo.

Move Around within a Document

Most documents are too big to be viewed in the window in their entirety. Here's how to get around your document quickly.

Notes:

- Moving your view of a document does not necessarily move the insertion point (see **Move Insertion Point**).

- Bookmarks can help you move to specific locations in a document.

- A Document Map provides an overview of a large, structured document. (See **Document Map**)

1 Use the Scroll bar buttons to move to where you desire:
- the end of the document
- the beginning of the document
- a specific part of the document (click and drag the square)

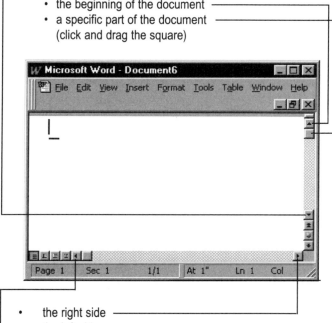

- the right side
- the left side

Move Around within a Document
continued . . .

Notes:

• Once an object is selected, you can use the next and previous page arrows to move from object to object.

• the previous page
• the next page

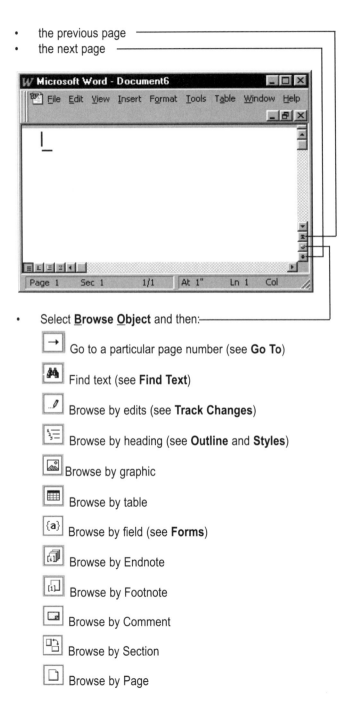

• Select **Browse Object** and then:—

→ Go to a particular page number (see **Go To**)

🔍 Find text (see **Find Text**)

✏️ Browse by edits (see **Track Changes**)

📋 Browse by heading (see **Outline** and **Styles**)

🖼️ Browse by graphic

▦ Browse by table

{a} Browse by field (see **Forms**)

📑 Browse by Endnote

📑 Browse by Footnote

🗨️ Browse by Comment

📑 Browse by Section

📄 Browse by Page

Scroll Using the Wheel on the Intellimouse

An Intellimouse has a wheel in the middle that can be used to scroll documents.

1 Roll the wheel to scroll up and down in the document
OR

Wheel-click the document window to change the vertical scroll bar.

2 Point above or below the center divider to scroll up or down in the document. The further you point from the center, the faster you scroll.

3 Wheel-click to go back to normal scrolling.

Move Insertion Point

The insertion point, which usually appears as a vertical line, can be placed on the page using the mouse or keystrokes.

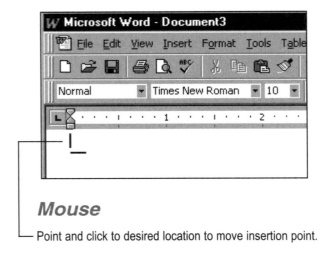

Mouse

Point and click to desired location to move insertion point.

Keystrokes

Moves the insertion point:	Press:
One character left	Left arrow
One character right	Right arrow
One line up	Up arrow
One line down	Down arrow
One word left	Ctrl + left arrow
One word right	Ctrl + right arrow
One paragraph up	Ctrl + up arrow
One paragraph down	Ctrl + down arrow
End of the line	End
Beginning of the line	Home
Top of the window	Alt + ctrl + page up
Bottom right of the window	Alt + ctrl + page down

Moves the insertion point:	Press:
Up one screen	Page up
Down one screen	Page down
Top of next page	Ctrl + page down
Top of previous page	Ctrl + page up
End of document	Ctrl + end
Beginning of document	Ctrl + home
Previous revision	Shift + F5
Location of insertion point when doc was last closed	Shift + F5

Tables

Moves the insertion point:	Press:
Next cell	Tab or right arrow
Previous cell	Shift + tab or left arrow
Previous row	Up arrow
Next row	Down arrow
First cell in row	Alt + home
Last cell in row	Alt + end
First cell in column	Alt + page up
Last cell in column	Alt + page down

New Document

New Document creates a new, blank file.

Notes:

- The keyboard shortcut for Create a New Document is Ctrl + N.

- New documents can be blank documents based on the Normal template, or they can be based on pre-formatted templates for memos, letters, facsimiles or other purposes. (See **Templates**).

- When Word is first started, a new document based on the Normal template automatically appears on the screen.

- New onscreen documents exist only in the computer's temporary RAM (Random Access Memory) until they are saved to a disk.

Toolbar

1 Click ☐.

2 A new, unnamed document based on the Normal template appears in the window.

Dialog Box

1 Click **File**, **New** to display the New dialog box.

2 Click the tab for the type of new document you wish to create.

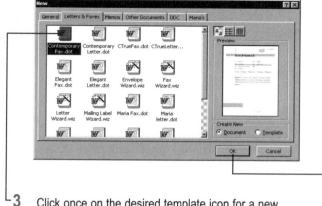

3 Click once on the desired template icon for a new document. A preview of the template appears in the Preview area.

4 Click **OK**.

Office Assistant

The Office Assistant provides context-sensitive help and allows you to type questions in plain English.

1 On the Standard toolbar, click the Office Assistant button
OR
Click **Help**, **Microsoft Word Help**.
The Office Assistant window appears.
OR
Double-Click on onscreen Office Assistant

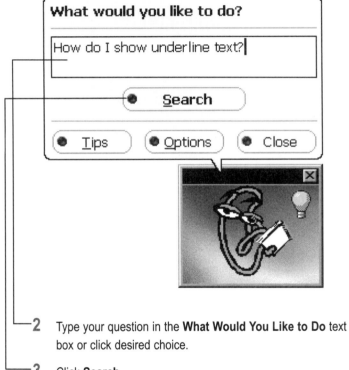

What would you like to do?

How do I show underline text?|

● **Search**

● **Tips**   ● **Options**   ● Close

2 Type your question in the **What Would You Like to Do** text box or click desired choice.

3 Click **Search**.

4 Complete the prompted instructions that follow to answer your questions in detail.

5 When you are finished, click **Esc** to close help options.

Choose Assistant

1 Right-click the Assistant window.

2 Click **Choose Assistant**.

3 Follow on-screen instructions.

Change Assistant Options

1 Right-click the Assistant window.

2 Click **Choose Assistant**.

3 Click the **Options** tab.

4 Click desired options.

Open Document

Opens a document file that has been previously saved on a disk.

Notes:

- The keyboard short-cut for opening a document is Ctrl + O.

- When you open a file of another format, such as a WordPerfect file or a file from a previous version of Word, Word will usually automatically convert the file to the Word 97 format.

- An open file automatically creates a temporary file in the current directory. When the document is correctly closed, the temporary file is deleted.

- Temporary Files are created to assist in restoring document resources, should a file be incorrectly closed.

1 Click **File**, **Open** to display the Open dialog box.

OR

Click .

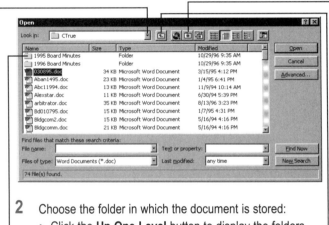

2 Choose the folder in which the document is stored:
- Click the **Up One Level** button to display the folders stored along with the folder currently displayed in the **Look in** text box.
- Double-click a folder icon in the list window to display the contents of that folder.
- Click the **Look in Favorites** button to display favorite folders that you have chosen.
- Click the **Look in** drop-down button to choose another disk drive or directory.

28

3 Choose how the list box displays your files:

• Click the **List** button to show as many files as possible.

• Click the **Details** button to show file information, such as size, type and date modified.

• Click the **Properties** button to show even more file information, including revision and printing history.

• Click the **Preview** button to display a thumbnail image of the file.

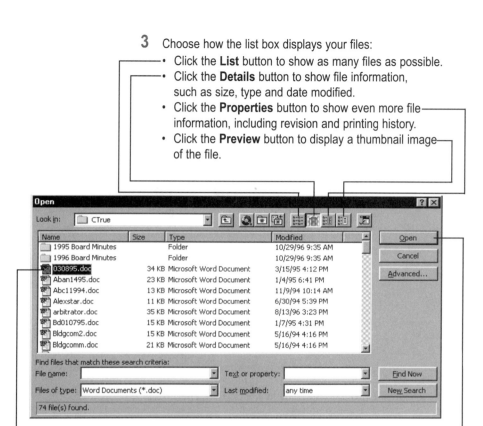

4 Click desired filename to open.

5 Click **Open**.

Options and Preferences

Many of the features and commands of Word are preset in specific ways. Use the Options dialog box to change the default settings and save your changes.

Notes:

- The Options dialog box is well worth exploring, especially after you have become familiar with Word and your own preferences and habits when using it.

1   Click **Tools**, **Options** to open the Options dialog box.

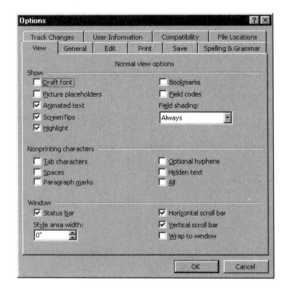

2   Click desired tab.

3   Change options as desired. To find out more about any particular option, right-click it, then click **What's this?**

4   Click **OK**.

Continue

→

Print a Document

The Print command sends the currently active document to the printer. Until they are printed, print jobs are stored in Print Manager.

Toolbar

Sends the document in the active window directly to the printer using the default printer settings. The Dialog Box options are not presented.

1   Click [🖨].

Dialog Box

1   Click **File**, **Print** to display the Print dialog box.

2   Click the **Name** drop down button to choose the desired printer.

3   Click the **Properties** button to change printer properties, such as print quality (options will vary depending on your printer).

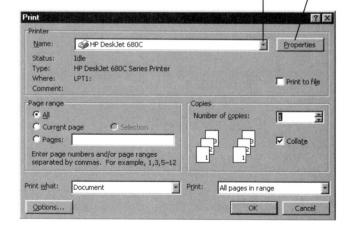

- Word enables you to print different page range combinations in a document. From the Print dialog box, click to select a page range:

All to print all the pages of the document.

Current page to print the page on which the insertion point is resting.

Selection to print currently selected text and graphics (must have been selected before dialog box was opened).

Pages to print desired page numbers (use a hyphen to specify a page range: 5-10; or use a commas to separate individual pages: 5,10).

4 Check a desired **Page Range** to print (see options in note box to the right).

5 Click **Number of copies** and type the desired number of copies to print.

6 Click **Print** drop-down button to print odd or even pages only.

7 Click **OK**.

Print Preview

Use Print Preview to see a screen view of exactly what your document will look like when printed.

- Print Previews will show you graphics, headers, footers and the margin area.

- Though you can adjust the margins while in Print Preview mode, you cannot edit the document contents.

1 Click
OR
Click **File**, **Print Preview**.

2 The pointer appears as a magnifying glass. Point and click the document image to see a close up view. Click again to view the entire page.

3 To see more than one page, click the **Multiple Page** button and drag across number of pages to see.

4 To see an image at an exact enlargement, click the **Zoom box** drop-down button and choose a size.

Notes:

- The ruler can be used to adjust page margins and indents and tabs (see **Margins**, **Tabs**, and **Indents**).

5 To display or hide the ruler, click the **View Ruler** button.

6 Click the **Shrink to Fit** button to adjust text to fit on one page.

7 Click the Full Screen button to increase the window size by removing all menu and scroll bars.

8 Click **Close** to return to the document window.

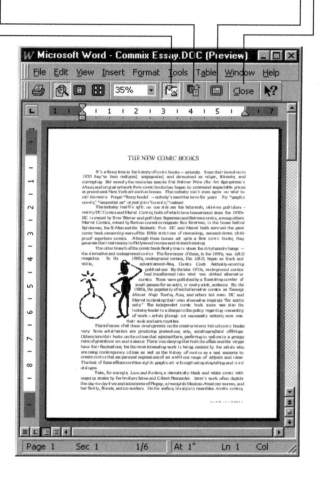

Save

Until a document has been saved to a disk, any changes that have been made to it exist only in the computer's temporary RAM.

1 Click **File**, **Save** to display the Save As dialog box.

OR

Click .

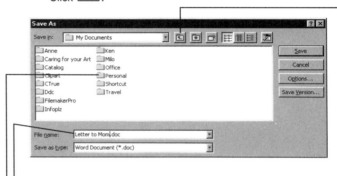

2 In the **File name** text box, type desired name of file (your typing will replace the default name).

3 Double-click the folder in which you want to place the document.

4 Click **Up One Level** button to display the folders stored along with the folder currently displayed in the Save in text box.

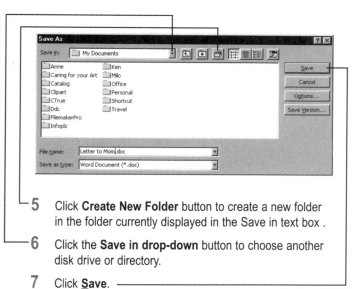

Notes:

- The first time you save a document, a Save As operation is performed by the computer (see **Save As**). This enables you to name the document for the first time and to indicate where you wish to save it. Each additional Save will simply save the most recent changes to the current document. The Save As dialog box will not reappear unless you choose Save As in place of Save.

5 Click **Create New Folder** button to create a new folder in the folder currently displayed in the Save in text box .

6 Click the **Save in drop-down** button to choose another disk drive or directory.

7 Click **S̲ave**. ⎯⎯⎯⎯⎯⎯⎯⎯⎯⎯⎯⎯⎯⎯

Save As

The Save As command is used to save an additional copy of a document with a different name or to a different directory or disk than the original document. (See also **Folders and Files**)

Notes:

- If you give a document the same name as an existing document and try to save it to the same folder, it will replace the original document.

- After you use the Save As command, the document in the active window is the most recently named one.

1 Click **File**, **Save As** to display the Save As dialog box.

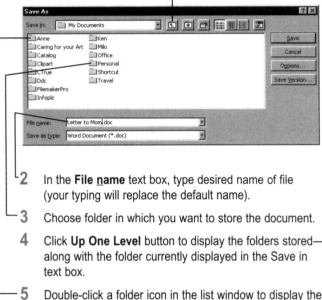

2 In the **File name** text box, type desired name of file (your typing will replace the default name).

3 Choose folder in which you want to store the document.

4 Click **Up One Level** button to display the folders stored along with the folder currently displayed in the Save in text box.

5 Double-click a folder icon in the list window to display the contents of that folder.

6 Click **Look in Favorites** button to display favorite folders that you have chosen.

7 Click **New Folder** button to create a new folder in the folder currently displayed in the Save in text box.

8 Click the **Save in** drop-down button to choose another disk drive.

9 Click **Save**.

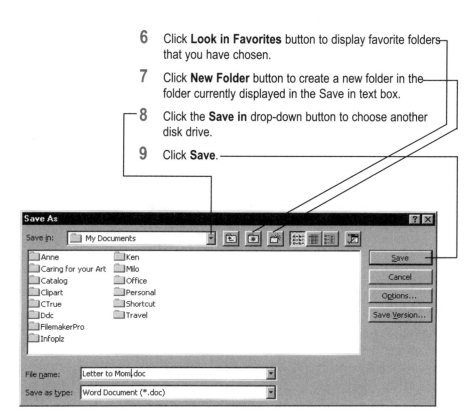

Select Text

Selecting text and graphics is one of the most basic actions used in word processing. Many commands and features are designed to affect only selected information.

Notes:

- When information is selected, it appears surrounded by a block of color that will depend on your Windows settings. Information can be selected a number of different ways using the mouse and the keyboard.

Mouse

Select this:	By doing this:
A varying amount of text and graphics	Click and drag over information.
A single word	Double-click the word.
A single graphic	Click the graphic.
A line of text	Click in the left margin (the pointer becomes an arrow).
Several lines of text	Click and drag in the left margin (the pointer becomes an arrow).
A sentence	Press Ctrl; click the sentence.
A paragraph	Double-click in the left margin (the pointer becomes an arrow) or triple-click the paragraph.
Several paragraphs	Double-click the left margin (the pointer becomes an arrow), then drag up or down.
A large amount of text and graphics	Click the beginning of the block, press and hold Shift, and click the end.
The entire document	Triple-click the left margin (the pointer becomes an arrow).
A vertical block of text	Press Alt, then click and drag over text.

Keyboard

Keyboard selections are relative to the current location of the insertion point.

Select this:	Press:
The character to the right	Shift + right arrow
The character to the left	Shift + left arrow
The rest of the word	Ctrl + shift + right arrow
The beginning of the word	Ctrl + shift + left arrow
The rest of the line	Shift + end
The beginning of the line	Shift + home
One line down	Shift + down arrow
One line up	Shift + up arrow
The rest of the paragraph	Ctrl + shift + down arrow
The beginning of the paragraph	Ctrl + shift + up arrow
One screen down	Shift + page down
One screen up	Shift + page up
The beginning of the document	Ctrl + shift + home
The entire document	Ctrl + A
A vertical block of text	Ctrl + shift + F8 + arrow keys, then esc to cancel
To exact locations	F8 + arrow keys, then esc to cancel

Select text and graphics in a table

Select this:	Press:
The next cell	Tab
The preceding cell	Shift + tab
Additional cells	Shift + desired arrow key
The column	Shift + up arrow or down arrow (repeat)
Additional columns or rows	Ctrl + shift + F8, esc to cancel
Fewer cells	Shift + F8
The entire table	Alt + 5 (numeric keypad only)

Show Invisible Codes

Word normally hides such formatting as paragraph markers, spaces, line returns and tabs. When you are formatting a document, however, it is sometimes helpful to display them.

Notes:

- The keyboard shortcut for showing Invisible codes is Ctrl + *.

- Invisible codes can be selected, then copied, cut or deleted just as other characters are.

Toolbar

1   On the Standard toolbar, click the Show/Hide button ¶.

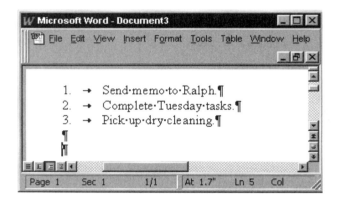

2   To hide codes, click ¶ again.

42

Dialog Box

1 Click **Tools**, **Options**.

2 Select to **View** tab in the Options Dialog Box.

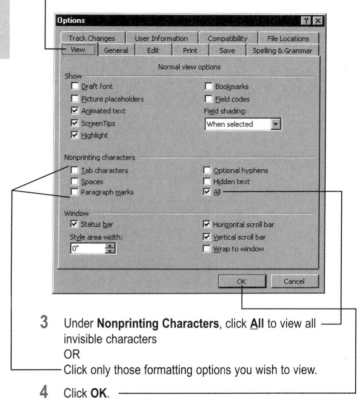

3 Under **Nonprinting Characters**, click **All** to view all invisible characters
OR
Click only those formatting options you wish to view.

4 Click **OK**.

Templates

Templates are special documents containing formatting and text that can be used as the basis for other documents.

Create a New Document Based on a Template

 File → New...

1 Click **File**, **New** to open the Templates dialog box.

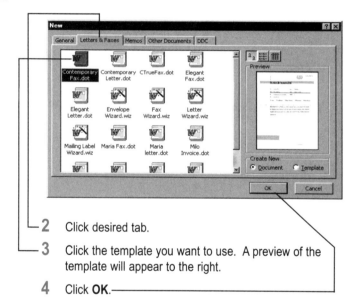

2 Click desired tab.

3 Click the template you want to use. A preview of the template will appear to the right.

4 Click **OK**.

Create a New Template

1 Click **File**, **New** to open the Templates dialog box.

2 Click desired tab.

3 Click template to use as base template.

4 Click **Template** option button.

5 Click **OK**.

6 Customize the template as desired.

7 Click Save button .

Name the template, making sure to retain the "dot" extension. Save the template in desired folder within the Templates folder (see **Folders and Files** for help with this task).

Toolbars

A toolbar, which is normally displayed below the menu bar, contains buttons that activate frequently used commands and features.

Notes:

• There are special-ized toolbars for dif-ferent kinds of tasks and different types of documents. These can be customized, or completely new custom toolbars can be created, named, and saved. You can also change toolbar options, such as button size and display of screen tips and shortcut keys.

Use a Toolbar

Point to the desired button and click
OR
point to any button and pause; a ToolTip will appear with a short description of the button.

Display a Toolbar

1 Right-click a displayed toolbar to display a list of all available toolbars
OR
Click **View**, **Toolbars.**

2 Click the toolbar you want to display.

Change Toolbar Options

1 Right-click a displayed toolbar
OR
Click **View**, **Toolbars**.

2 Click **Customize**. The Customize dialog box appears.

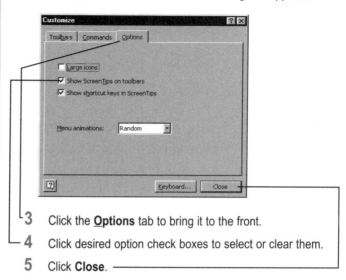

3 Click the **Options** tab to bring it to the front.

4 Click desired option check boxes to select or clear them.

5 Click **Close**.

Create a New Toolbar

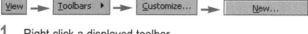

1 Right-click a displayed toolbar
   OR
   Click **View**, **Toolbars**.

2 Click **Customize**. Click the **Toolbars** tab.

3 Click **New**.

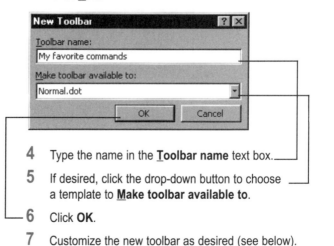

4 Type the name in the **Toolbar name** text box.

5 If desired, click the drop-down button to choose a template to **Make toolbar available to**.

6 Click **OK**.

7 Customize the new toolbar as desired (see below).

Toolbars *continued . . .*

A toolbar, which is normally displayed below the menu bar, contains buttons that activate frequently used commands and features.

Notes:

- You can receive help from the Office Assistant while customizing your toolbar by clicking the Help button in the bottom right corner of the Customize dialog box.

Customize Toolbar

View → Toolbars ▶ → Customize...

1 Right-click a displayed toolbar

OR

Click **View**, **Toolbars**.

2 Click **Customize**. The Customize dialog box appears.

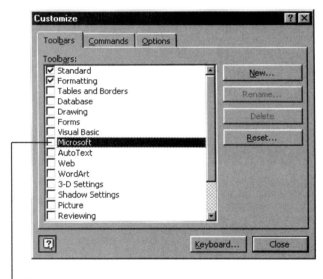

3 If it is not already displayed, click the checkbox of the toolbar to customize.

4 Click the **Commands** tab.

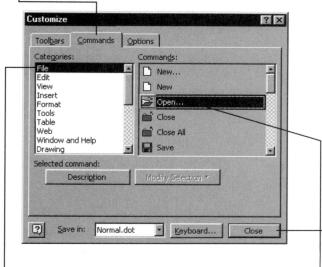

5 In the **Categories** list box, click desired category of command or feature.

6 In the **Commands** list box, click and drag desired command to the toolbar. A "+" displayed at the insertion point indicates that the button can be placed at the current location. An "X" indicates that the insertion point is not yet placed on a toolbar.

7 To remove a button, click and drag it from the toolbar. Drop it anywhere.

8 When finished, click **Close**.

View Document

Your document can be viewed in several ways, which reveal different structural aspects.

Normal View

At the bottom left corner of the document window, click

OR

Click **View**, **Normal**.

Online Layout View

At the bottom left corner of the document window, click

OR

Click **View**, **Online Layout**.

Page Layout View

At the bottom left corner of the document window, click

OR

Click **View**, **Page Layout**.

Print Preview

 →

Click

OR

Click **File**, **Print Preview**.

Master Document View

View → Master Document

Click **View**, **Master Document**.

51

Zoom View

Use Zoom to enlarge or reduce your view of the document in the document window without changing actual text size.

Notes:

- You can open a second window on a document to view two different magnification sizes at once (see **Arrange Windows**).

- Zoom View does not affect the print size of the document.

Toolbar

Click the Zoom drop-down button 100% and click desired size to view.

Dialog Box

1 Click **View**, **Zoom** to open the Zoom dialog box.

2 Check box for desired viewing size.
OR
Click **Percent** text box and type desired percentage.

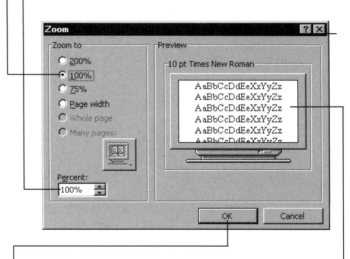

3 When size is chosen, a preview of page size and text will appear in the Preview window of the Zoom Dialog Box.

4 Click **OK**.

Format Character

This section will demonstrate different methods of enhancing text. You will learn to change font size and appearance, create drop capitals, and arrange text into columns. You will also learn to use the Format Painter to copy formatting from one place to another, and to make use of bullets, symbols and special characters.

Align Text

Text can be aligned at the left or right margins, evenly justified between margins, or centered along a vertical axis.

Notes:

- The keyboard shortcuts for aligning text are:

  Left: Ctrl + L

  Right: Ctrl + R

  Justified: Ctrl + J

  Centered: Ctrl + E

Toolbar

1 Click and drag over text to format.

OR

Point to and click the spot where you plan to type new text.

2 Click desired toolbar button:

- **Left align** button

- **Right align** button

- **Justify** (left and right align) button

- **Center align** button

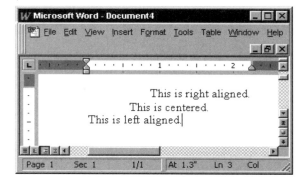

54

Dialog Box

1 Click and drag over text to format.
OR
Point to and click the spot where you plan to type new text.

2 Click **Format**, **Paragraph** to display the Paragraph dialog box.

3 Click the **Indents and Spacing** tab.

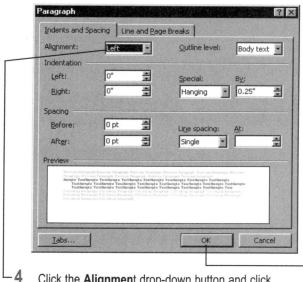

4 Click the **Alignment** drop-down button and click desired alignment.

5 Click **OK** ───────────────────────

55

Bullets

A variety of bullet shapes can be used to indicate items on a list.

Toolbar

1   Click and drag over items to bullet
    OR
    Point to and click the spot where you plan to type the list.

2   Click the Bullets button .

3   Type the list, pressing the **Enter** key between each item.

4   When you are finished, click the Bullets button again to deselect.

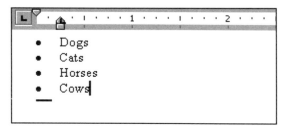

Keyboard Shortcuts

1   Press the **hyphen** or **asterisk** key followed by the **Tab** key.

2   Type the first item on the list.

3   Press the **Enter** key. The next bullet will appear (to format other bullet shapes, see below).

4   To quit bulleting, press the **Backspace** key to delete the last tab and number.
    OR
    Press **Enter**, **Enter**.

Format Bullets

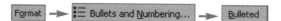

The bullet style can be customized using the Format Bullets command.

1 Click and drag over bulleted list.
OR
Point to and click the spot where you plan to type a bulleted list.

2 Click **Format**, **Bullets and Numbering** to display the Bullets and Numbering dialog box.
OR
Right-click the list; click **Bullets and Numbering**.

3 If necessary, click the **Bulleted** tab to bring it to the front.

4 Click the desired bullet style.

5 Click **OK**.

Change Case

The Change Case command changes text from upper case to lower case, or vice versa, and also has the capacity to capitalize only selected letters.

Notes:

- Sentence case capitalizes the first word following a period. Title case capitalizes every word. Toggle case switches case for each letter.

1 Click and drag over text to select it.

2 Click **Format**, **Change Case** to open the dialog box.

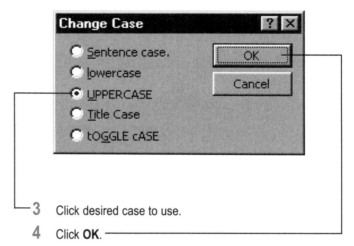

3 Click desired case to use.

4 Click **OK**.

58

Characters: Symbol and Special

Most commonly used characters are found on the standard keyboard. But other symbols and characters, such as foreign characters, foreign money symbols, copyright symbols are also available to use.

Notes:

- Some symbols are available using the AutoCorrect feature.

- Different symbols and characters are available for each font.

1   Click **Insert**, **Symbol**. The Symbol dialog box opens.

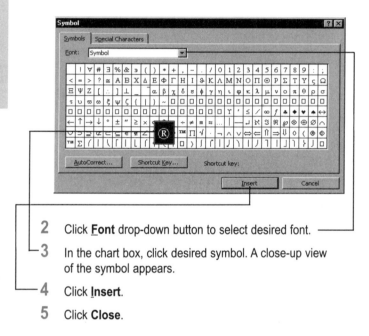

2   Click **Font** drop-down button to select desired font.

3   In the chart box, click desired symbol. A close-up view of the symbol appears.

4   Click **Insert**.

5   Click **Close**.

Columns

The Columns feature can be used to format any number and size of columns, depending on the width of your paper. You can create columns by using the toolbar and ruler, or by using the dialog box.

Notes:

- To create columns with items that align horizontally, create a table (see Table).

- To add vertical lines between columns, click the checkbox in the Columns dialog box. To see the lines, view your document in Page Layout View or Print Preview (see **View Document**).

Toolbar

Click and hold Columns button, then drag across number of columns desired.

Dialog Box

1 Point to and click where you want to start typing text in columns.
OR
Select text to be formatted in columns.

2 Click **Format**, **Columns** to open the Columns dialog box.

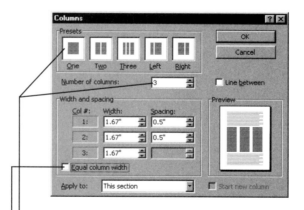

3 Click desired number of columns in the **Presets** area.
OR
Click **Number of columns** text box and type desired number.

4 Check or clear **Equal column width** box, as desired.

5 Change column **Width**, as desired.

6 Change **Spacing** between columns, as desired.

7 Click **OK** when you are finished.

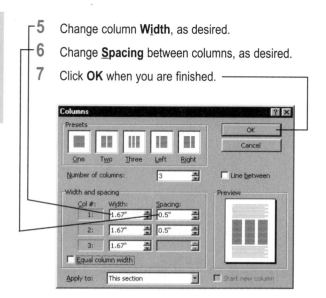

Change Column Width and Spacing

Column spacing can be easily changed by either using the ruler or accessing the Columns dialog box.

1 If necessary, click **View**, **Ruler** to display the ruler.

2 Click and drag edges of columns to change column width or spacing.

3 Change indents as with regular text (see **Indent Paragraphs**).

Start a New Column

Use a Column Break to begin typing at the top of a new column.

1 Click **Insert**, **Break** to open the Break dialog box.

2 Click **Column break** button.

3 Click **OK**.

61

Drop Cap

A drop cap is a decorative first letter of a paragraph.

Notes:

- The Distance from text measurement determines the space between the drop cap and the next letter in the word.

- To remove a drop cap, select None in the Drop Cap dialog box.

1   Point to and click the paragraph to begin with a drop cap.

2   Click **Format**, **Drop Cap** to open the Drop Cap dialog box.

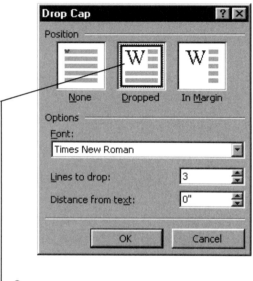

3   Click desired **Position** of drop cap.

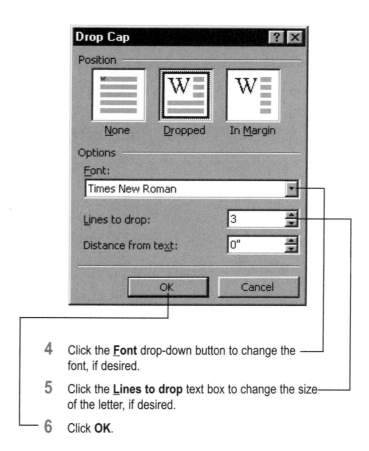

4 Click the **Font** drop-down button to change the font, if desired.

5 Click the **Lines to drop** text box to change the size of the letter, if desired.

6 Click **OK**.

Font

Format font changes the typeface, the style (such as bold or italic), the size, color and other aspects of the type in your documents.

Notes:

- Font attributes can be changed one at a time using the toolbar, or all can be accessed at once using the Font dialog box. The Font dialog box also contains additional attributes that are not available on the toolbar.

Toolbar

1   Click and drag over text to format.
    OR
    Point to and click the spot where you plan to type new text.

2   To change the typeface, click the Font drop-down button
    `Times New Roman  ▼` and click desired font.

3   To change font size, click the Font Size drop-down button
    `10  ▼` and click desired size.

4   To make font bold, click the Bold button `B`.

5   To make font italicized, click the Italics button `I`.

6   To underline text, click the Underline button `U`.

7   To change text color, click the arrow next to the

    Font Color drop down button `A ▾`.

Font Dialog Box

1   Select text to format
    OR
    Point to and click the spot where you plan to type new text.

2 Click **Format**, **Font** to display the Font dialog box.

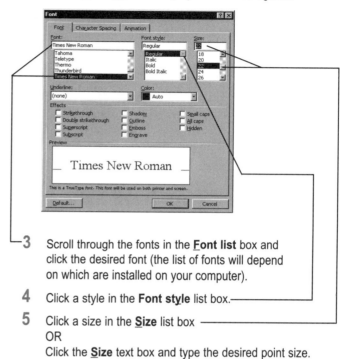

3 Scroll through the fonts in the **Font list** box and click the desired font (the list of fonts will depend on which are installed on your computer).

4 Click a style in the **Font style** list box.

5 Click a size in the **Size** list box
OR
Click the **Size** text box and type the desired point size.

6 Click **Underline** drop-down button to select desired underline style.

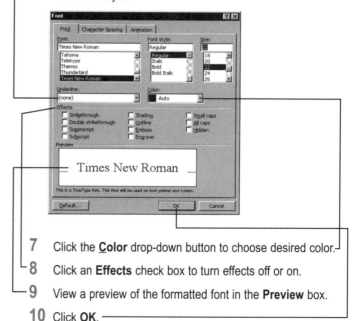

7 Click the **Color** drop-down button to choose desired color.

8 Click an **Effects** check box to turn effects off or on.

9 View a preview of the formatted font in the **Preview** box.

10 Click **OK**.

65

Format Painter

The Format Painter copies all character and paragraph formatting from selected text and applies it to text you specify.

Notes:

- The keyboard shortcut for activating the Format Painter is **Ctrl + Shift + C.**

- The Format Painter is only available from the toolbar and shortcut keys.

1 Click and drag to select the text with the formatting you would like to copy.

2 Click once on the Format Painter button .

3 Click and drag over text to format.

To paint the same format more than once:

1 Click and drag to select the text with the formatting you would like to copy.

2 Double-click the Format Painter button .

3 Click and drag over each text section to format.

4 Click the Format Painter button to turn painting off.

Format Pages

This section will introduce formatting options that will make your documents more organized and visually appealing. You will learn how to set tabs, margins, headers and footers, and how to number pages and lists. In addition, you will learn how to vary spacing within your document and how to create an outline.

Footnotes and Endnotes

Word automatically numbers and renumbers footnotes and endnotes when notes are added to or deleted from the text.

1 Point and click to place insertion point at referenced text.

2 Click **Insert**, **Footnote** to open the Footnote and Endnote dialog box.

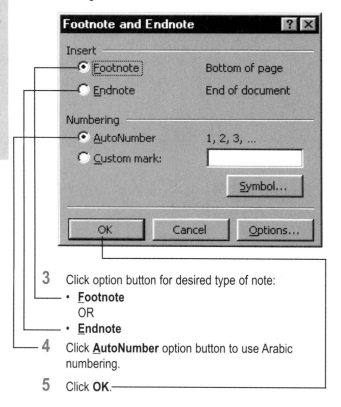

3 Click option button for desired type of note:
- **Footnote**
  OR
- **Endnote**

4 Click **AutoNumber** option button to use Arabic numbering.

5 Click **OK**.

6 The Footnote or Endnote pane appears. Type desired text.

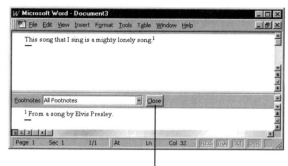

7 When finished click **Close**.

View footnote or endnote text

Point to desired footnote or endnote number. The note text will appear in a small window near the pointer.

Edit footnote or endnote text

1 Point to footnote or endnote number to edit and double-click.

2 In the Footnote or Endnote pane, make desired changes.

3 Click **Close**.

Delete a footnote or endnote

1 Click and drag over superscript number in the body text of the document to select it.

2 Press **Del**.

Move a footnote or endnote

1 Click and drag over superscript number in the body text of the document to select it.

2 On the toolbar, click **Cut** button ✄, or use any alternative cut, copy or move command.

3 Click desired new location in body text.

4 On the toolbar, click **Paste** button 📋, or use any alternative paste command.

Headers and Footers

Headers and footers are used to contain text that will repeat at the top or bottom of consecutive pages. Headers and footers can include page numbers, dates, filenames, and other specialized information.

Notes:

- To quickly edit a header or footer, view the document in Page Layout View, then double-click the header or footer.

- When you edit a header or footer, it changes throughout the entire document.

1 Click **View**, **Header and Footer**. The header and footer areas appear and the header and footer toolbar is displayed.

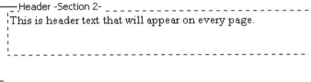

2 Type text to repeat in the header or footer area defined by the dotted line. Use the toolbar buttons to include special information where desired:

- Page number button 🔳

- Number of pages button 🔳

- Format page number button 🔳

- Date button 🔳

- Time button 🔳

3 When finished, click `Close`.

Change Header or Footer

1   View the page where you want the new header or footer to begin to appear.

2   Insert a section break by clicking **Insert**, **Break** and choosing desired break (see **Section Breaks**).

3   If necessary, click **View**, **Header and Footer** to display the header and footer areas.

4   On the header and footer toolbar, click .

5   Type the desired new header or footer.

Edit Header or Footer

1   If necessary, click **View**, **Header and Footer** to display the header and footer areas.

2   Click in header or footer area and edit text as desired.

3   Click **Close**.

Indent Paragraphs

Paragraphs can be quickly indented from the left using the toolbar buttons. Using the Paragraph dialog box, you can also set paragraphs with only the first line indented or with all lines following the first indentation (a hanging indent).

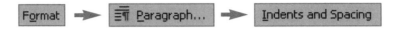

Notes:

- Click the Increase Indent button repeatedly to move text further to the right.

- A paragraph with a hanging indent has all lines after the first line indented on the left.

Toolbar

1   Click and drag over paragraphs to indent
OR
Point to and click the spot where you plan to type new paragraphs.

2   Click **Increase Indent** button to move text to the right
OR

Click **Decrease Indent** button to move text to the left.

Change Indentation Spacing

1   If necessary, click **View**, **Ruler** to display the ruler.

2   Click and drag the first line indent marker to change the first line of text.

3   Click and drag the left indent marker to change the indent for the rest of the lines in the paragraph.

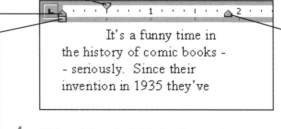

4   Click and drag the left indent box to change the indent for all lines of text.

5   Click and drag the right indent box to change the right indent.

Dialog Box

1 Click and drag over paragraphs to indent.
OR
Point to and click the spot where you plan to type new paragraphs.

2 Click **Format**, **Paragraph** to display the Paragraph dialog box.

3 If necessary, click the **Indents and Spacing** tab to bring it to the front.

4 Click the **Left** text box and type desired distance to indent from the left margin.

5 Click **Right** text box and type the desired distance to indent from the right margin.

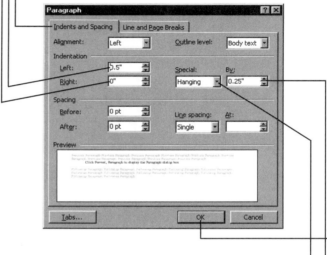

6 Click the **Special** drop-down button and click the desired indent type.

7 Click the **By** text box and type distance for special indenting from the left margin.

8 Click **OK**.

73

Insert Date and Time

The Date and Time feature automatically inserts the current date and time into your document.

Notes:

- The date and time can be formatted in a number of ways and can be automatically updated, if necessary.

1 Click **Insert**, **Date and Time**. The Date and Time dialog box opens

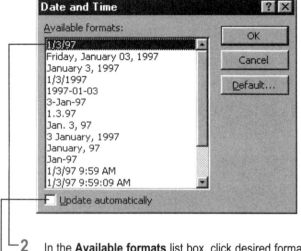

2 In the **Available formats** list box, click desired format.

3 To have the date or time update automatically each time the document is opened, click the **Update automatically** checkbox.

Continue

→

Numbering a List

Word will automatically number a list and, if items are moved or added, automatically renumber the list will automatically be renumbered. The number format can be controlled separately.

Notes:

• Document
outlines can also
be numbered.
(See **Outline**).

1   Press the 1 key followed by a period (.). Press the **Tab** key.

2   Type the first item on the list.

3   Press the **Enter** key. The next number will appear.

4   To quit numbering, press the **Backspace** key to delete
the last tab and number.
OR
Press **Enter**, **Enter**.

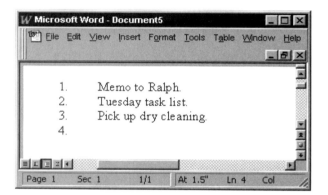

Toolbar

1   Click and drag over items to number
OR
Point to and click the spot where you plan to type the list.

2   Click the Numbering button ▣.

3   Type the list, pressing the **Enter** key between items.

4   When finished, click the Numbering button ▣.

Notes:

- To remove numbering, choose None in the Bullets and Numbering dialog box.

Edit Numbering

An automatically numbered list can be edited in various ways.

Add a New Numbered Item

1   Click the end of the previous item and press **Enter**.

2   Type the new item (the numbers will automatically adjust).

Move a Numbered Item

1   Click and drag the margin to the left of the items to highlight them.

2   Click and drag the items to the new location (the numbers will automatically adjust).

Delete Numbered Items

1   Click and drag the margin to the left of the items to highlight them.

2   Press **Delete** or **Backspace** (the numbers will automatically adjust).

Extend Numbering

Use when continuing a number series after a text interruption.

1   Click and drag over list to add to number series.

2   Click **F**ormat, **Bullets and** **N**umbering to display the Bullets and Numbering dialog box.
    OR
    Right-click the highlight, click **Bullets and** **N**umbering.

3   Click **C**ontinue Previous List.

4   Click **OK**.

Numbering a List *continued . . .*

Word will automatically number a list and, if items are moved or added, the list will automatically be renumbered. The number format can be controlled separately (see **Format Numbering**).

Notes:

- To renumber a list beginning with a new or non-sequential order, right-click the item in the list where renumbering is to begin and do the following:
  Click Bullets and Numbering, click Customize, and type the new desired number in the Start at text box. The remaining items in the list will be renumber as well.

Restart Numbering

Use to renumber a section of a list, restarting from one(1).

1 Click and drag over section of list to renumber.

2 Click **Format**, **Bullets and Numbering** to display the Bullets and Numbering dialog box.
OR
Right-click the highlight, click **Bullets and Numbering**.

3 Click **Restart Numbering**.

4 Click **OK**.

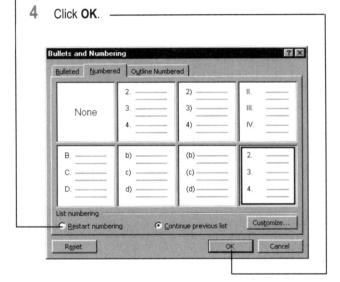

78

Format Numbering

The number style and type for lists that are automatically numbered by Word can be customized using the Format Numbering command.

1 Click and drag over numbered list.
OR
Point to and click the spot where you plan to type a numbered list.

2 Click **Format**, **Bullets and Numbering** to display the Bullets and Numbering dialog box.
OR
Right-click the list to change, click **Bullets and Numbering**.

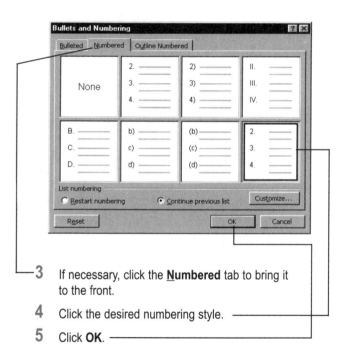

3 If necessary, click the **Numbered** tab to bring it to the front.

4 Click the desired numbering style.

5 Click **OK**.

Margin Settings

Page margins can be quickly changed using the ruler or they can be set to precise locations by using the dialog box.

Ruler

1 If necessary, switch to Page Layout view ☰ (the button is at the lower left corner of the document window) OR

Switch to Print Preview 🔍.

2 If necessary, click **View**, **Ruler** to display the rulers.

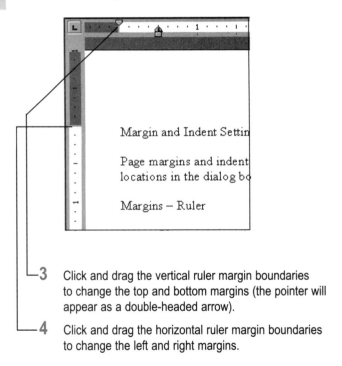

3 Click and drag the vertical ruler margin boundaries to change the top and bottom margins (the pointer will appear as a double-headed arrow).

4 Click and drag the horizontal ruler margin boundaries to change the left and right margins.

Dialog Box

1   If necessary, select section of text for which you want to change margins.

2   Click **File**, **Page Setup**, **Margins** to view the Margins tab of the Page Setup dialog box.

3   Type desired margin width in the appropriate **Margins** text boxes (a preview will appear to the right).

4   Type desired **Header and Footer** margins in the **From Edge** text boxes.

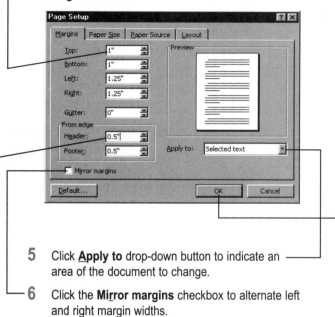

5   Click **Apply to** drop-down button to indicate an area of the document to change.

6   Click the **Mirror margins** checkbox to alternate left and right margin widths.

7   Click **OK**.

Outline

Outline view allows you to easily create and edit an outline to which text and graphics can be added later.

1 At the bottom left corner of the document window,

click the Outline View button [⬛]
OR
Click **View**, **Outline**. The first outline symbol, a minus sign(-) appears.

2 Type the first heading and press Enter. A second outline symbol appears beneath the first.

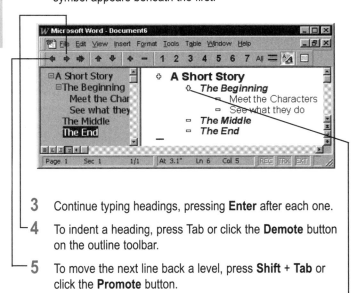

3 Continue typing headings, pressing **Enter** after each one.

4 To indent a heading, press Tab or click the **Demote** button on the outline toolbar.

5 To move the next line back a level, press **Shift** + **Tab** or click the **Promote** button.

6 Headings with subheadings beneath them have a plus sign (+) as an outline symbol.

Notes:

- To create an outline without using built-in heading styles, create a numbered list and set the number format to the outline style of your choice (see **Numbering**).
- The Outlining toolbar is available only in Outline view.

7 To move a heading to another part of the document, click and drag its outline symbol up or down. Any subheadings will move with it.

8 To change the level of a heading or subheading, click and drag its outline symbol to the left or right.

9 When you are finished, at the bottom left corner of the document window:

Click the Normal View button or the Page Layout View button
OR
Click **View**, **Normal** or **Page Layout**
to add body text and graphics to the document.

Page Numbering

Use the Page Numbers command to add page numbers to the top or bottom of your document pages.

Notes:

- For more elaborate page numbering, insert a page number field in the document header or footer.

- Hide the page number on the first page by clearing the Show number on first page check box in the Page Numbers dialog box.

1 Click **Insert**, **Page Numbers** to display the Page Numbers dialog box.

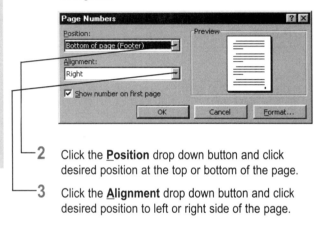

2 Click the **Position** drop down button and click desired position at the top or bottom of the page.

3 Click the **Alignment** drop down button and click desired position to left or right side of the page.

- Begin numbering
  after the first
  document page by
  typing a number in
  the Start at text box
  on the Page Number
  Format dialog box.

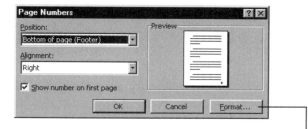

4   To change the default number format or to start page
    numbering at a number other than one or two, click the
    Format button to display the Page Number Format
    dialog box.

- Click the **Number format** drop down button
  and click desired number format to use.
- Click the **Start at** text box and type the desired
  beginning page number in the text box.
- Click **OK**.

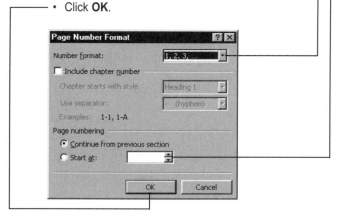

5   In the Page Numbering dialog box, click **OK**.

Paragraph and Line Spacing

Word allows you to set different spacing between paragraphs and lines of text.

Notes:

- When you press the Enter key, you are telling Word that you are beginning a new paragraph. If you want to begin a new line of text without starting a new paragraph, press Shift+Enter.

- To see paragraph end markers, click the Show/Hide button on the toolbar.

- There are 72 points in an inch.

1 Point and click where you intend to type text with new spacing
OR
Click and drag over text to change spacing

2 Click **Format**, **Paragraph** to open the Paragraph dialog box.

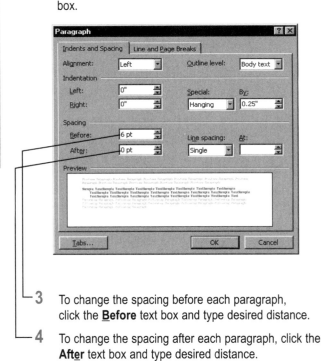

3 To change the spacing before each paragraph, click the **Before** text box and type desired distance.

4 To change the spacing after each paragraph, click the **After** text box and type desired distance.

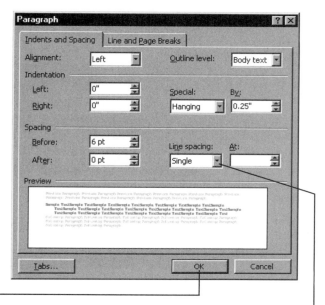

5 To change the spacing between all lines, click the **Line** spacing drop-down button and choose desired spacing:
- **Single** for closely spaced lines
- **Double** to alternate blank lines with text lines
- **At least** to enter a minimum point distance in the At text box
- **Exactly** to enter a point distance in the At text box
- **Multiple** to add more than one blank line between each line of text

6 When finished, click **OK**.

Ruler

The rulers are used to measure the position of text on the page, and can also be used to set margins, indents, and tabs.

Notes:

- In Normal view, only the horizontal ruler is displayed. Switch to Page Layout view to see the vertical ruler.

Display or Hide Ruler

Click **View**, **Ruler** (a check mark next to the menu choice indicates that it is currently displayed).

Continue

→

Section Breaks

Section breaks are used when you wish to apply margins, headers and footers, protection, or other formatting to only part of a document.

Insert a Section Break

1 Click location where section break will occur.

2 Click **Insert**, **Break** to open the Break dialog box.

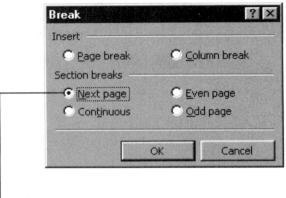

3 Click desired type of break:
- **Next page** to insert a combination section break and page break.
- **Continuous** to begin the new section at the current location.
- **Even page** or **Odd page** to begin the new section at the next specified page.

4 Click **OK**.

Delete a Section Break

1   If section breaks are not visible, click the

Show/Hide button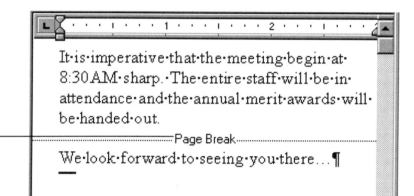

2   Click and drag over the visible page break.

3   Press the **Delete** key.

It·is·imperative·that·the·meeting·begin·at·
8:30 AM·sharp.·The·entire·staff·will·be·in·
attendance·and·the·annual·merit·awards·will·
be·handed·out.
——————————————————Page Break——————————————————
We·look·forward·to·seeing·you·there…¶

Tabs

Use tabs to align text precisely on the page. Tabs can be used to left align, center align, right align, or decimal align text.

Notes:

- Tab settings can be placed using the ruler, or by accessing the Tabs dialog box additional options. (If ruler is not visible, click View, Rule.)

- Because word processor applications do not read space markings in the same way that typewriters do, do not use the space bar to attempt to align text or objects on a page. What looks aligned onscreen will most likely not print the same way. Always use tabs and indent markers to align your document. Be sure to double check the final outcome in Print Preview.

- To align text more than one way on a single line, use tabs.

- To make lines closer to the same length (less ragged), change the hyphenation zone (see **Hyphenation**).

Ruler

1 Click and drag over text to be affected by tab sets.
   OR
   Point to and click the spot where you plan to type and tab new text.

2 Point to and click desired location on the bottom edge of the ruler. A tab symbol will appear.

3 Point to and click the **Tab** button at left edge of ruler until desired tab appears:

   - **Left align** text at tab
   - **Center** text on tab
   - **Right align** text at tab
   - **Decimal align** text at tab

4 To move a tab, click and drag its symbol to a new location on the ruler.

5 To remove a tab, click and drag its symbol off the ruler.

Dialog Box

1 Click and drag over text to be affected by tab sets.
OR
Point and click to the spot where you plan to type and tab new text.

2 Click **Format**, **Tabs** to display the Tabs dialog box.

3 Type the desired tab location in the **Tab stop position** text box (the default tab alignment is relative to the left margin).

4 Click the desired **Alignment** radio button.

5 Click the desired **Leader** radio button.

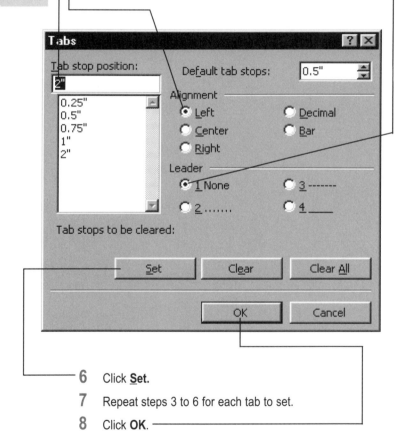

6 Click **Set**.

7 Repeat steps 3 to 6 for each tab to set.

8 Click **OK**.

Editing Information

This section will help you to make changes and additions to your documents. Some of the most common actions in word processing are moving and copying text. You will be able to find and replace text easily, set bookmarks, and create keystroke shortcuts for specified text. You will learn to make use of Word's correction tools to assist with spelling and grammar. Word also provides you with easy methods of creating summaries and adding comments, as well as inserting files into master documents.

AutoCorrect

The AutoCorrect feature fixes common typographical errors and replaces specific keystrokes with special characters automatically. It can be customized as desired.

Tools ➡ AutoCorrect...

Notes:

- AutoCorrect can be used to replace your own personal abbreviations with the spelled out words that they represent.

- Scroll the top of the list box in the AutoCorrect dialog to learn character combinations that will be replaced with common symbols.

Change AutoCorrect Settings

1 Click **Tools**, **AutoCorrect** to open the AutoCorrect dialog box.

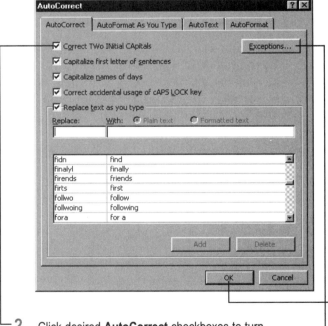

2 Click desired **AutoCorrect** checkboxes to turn options on or off.

3 Click **Exceptions** button to add exceptions to the rules.

4 When finished, click **OK**.

96

Add New AutoCorrect Entry

1 In document window, select word, symbol or graphic that will replace text.

2 Click **Tools**, **AutoCorrect** to open the AutoCorrect dialog box. The selection appears in the **With** text box.

3 Click the **Replace** text box and type text.

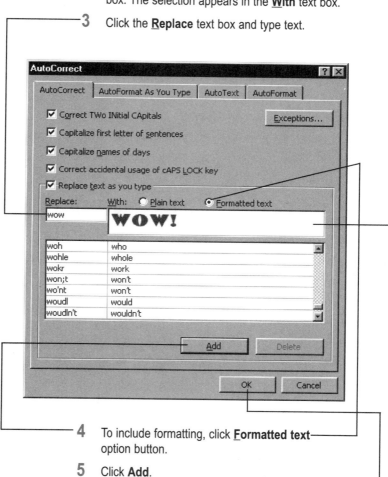

4 To include formatting, click **Formatted text** option button.

5 Click **Add**.

6 Click **OK**.

AutoSummarize

The AutoSummarize feature selects key text and analyzes it based on frequently used words and sentence structure.

Notes:

- AutoSummarize works best on formally structured documents.

- AutoSummarize adds to the key words and comments boxes of the document properties. To avoid replacing your own key words and comments, clear the Update document statistics checkbox in the AutoSummarize dialog box.

1 View document to be summarized.
OR
Select text to be summarized.

2 Click **Tools**, **AutoSummarize** to open the AutoSummarize dialog box.

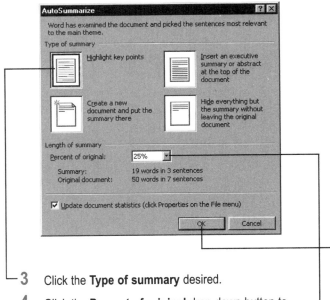

3 Click the **Type of summary** desired.

4 Click the **Percent of original** drop-down button to use more or fewer sentences.

5 Click **OK** to highlight or copy summary text. If **Highlight key points** or **Hide everything but the summary** is chosen, the AutoSummarize toolbar appears.

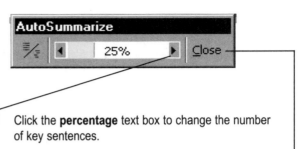

6   Click the **percentage** text box to change the number
     of key sentences.

7   Click **C**lose to remove highlighting or display the
     original document.

AutoText

The AutoText feature stores frequently used text and graphics, which can be chosen from a list of AutoText entries, or which may be accessed and inserted into text by typing shortcut keys. You can create your own AutoText entries for any amount of text or for any graphic object.

Notes:

- AutoText entries are linked to the paragraph style of the text or graphic stored in the entry.

- AutoText entries are stored with the Normal template and are available to all documents, unless you specify a template to store the entry in.

- When you are creating many AutoText entries at one time, use the AutoText toolbar (see **Toolbars**).

Create an AutoText Entry

1   Select text and graphics to save as AutoText.

2   Click **Insert**, **AutoText**, **New**. The Create AutoText dialog box opens.

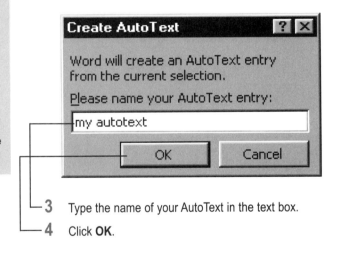

3   Type the name of your AutoText in the text box.

4   Click **OK**.

Insert AutoText

1　Point to and click the desired location to place AutoText.

2　Click **Insert**, **A̲utoText**. A submenu of AutoText choices appears.

3　Click desired submenu to see another submenu of choices. Click desired AutoText choice.

　OR

1　Point to and click the desired location to place AutoText.

2　Type AutoText name.

3　Press **F3**. The AutoText is retrieved.

Bookmarks

A bookmark is used to add a named place holder to a significant section of a document. Once it is added, you can return easily to that section at any time.

Notes:

- The keyboard shortcut for creating a Bookmark is Ctrl + G.

- You can use the scroll bar to move from bookmark to bookmark (see **Move Around within a Document**).

- Make bookmarks visible by changing the setting on the View tab of the Options dialog box. (see **Options and Preferences**).

1   Point to and click the desired location for placing a bookmark.

2   Click **Insert**, **Bookmark** to open the Bookmark dialog box.

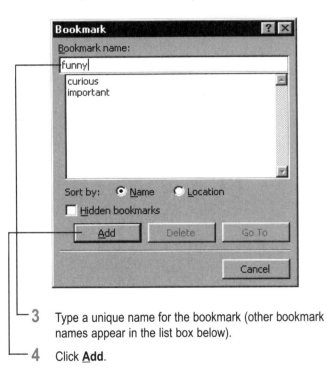

3   Type a unique name for the bookmark (other bookmark names appear in the list box below).

4   Click **Add**.

Go to a Bookmark

To access a bookmark once it has been created, do the following:

1 Click **Edit**, **Go To** to open the Go To dialog box.
OR
Press **Ctrl + G**.

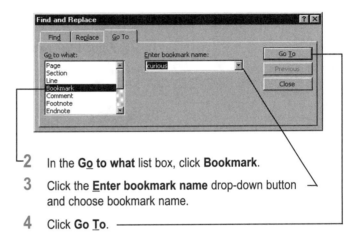

2 In the **Go to what** list box, click **Bookmark**.

3 Click the **Enter bookmark name** drop-down button and choose bookmark name.

4 Click **Go To**.

Delete a Bookmark

1 Click **Insert**, **Bookmark** to open the Bookmark dialog box.

2 In the Bookmark name list box, click desired bookmark to delete.

3 Click the **Delete** key.

4 When finished, click **Close**.

103

Comment

You can use comments on a Word document just as you use sticky notes on a paper document. The text you comment on is highlighted and when you point to it, the comment appears.

1 Click and drag over text to comment on.

2 Click **Insert**, **Comment** to open the Comment pane.

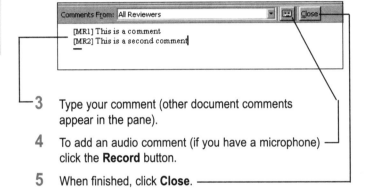

3 Type your comment (other document comments appear in the pane).

4 To add an audio comment (if you have a microphone) click the **Record** button.

5 When finished, click **Close**.

Edit a Comment

1 Right-click the comment to display the shortcut menu.

2 Click **Edit Comment**.

Delete a Comment

1 Right-click the comment to display the shortcut menu.

2 Click **Delete Comment**.

```
  ✂  Cut
  ▣  Copy
  📋 Paste
  ─────────────────
  🖉 Edit Comment
  🗙 Delete Comment
  ─────────────────
  A  Font...
  ≡¶ Paragraph...
  ⫶≡ Bullets and Numbering...
  ─────────────────
     Define
```

Review Comments

1 Right-click the toolbar and choose **Reviewing** to display the Reviewing Toolbar it.

2 Click **Next Comment** button
Or
Previous Comment button to move from comment to comment.

Copy Information

Use the Copy command to copy text, formatting and graphics and to place them elsewhere in the document, or into a different document. Because it is such a common word processing task, there are several ways to copy information.

Notes:

- The keyboard short-cut for copying information is Ctrl + C.

- Word's drag-and-drop feature must be turned on in order to copy text with the Ctrll key (as mentioned in step 1). To turn the drag-and-drop text feature on, click Tools, Options, and check the Drag-and-drop text editing option.

- Copied information is placed on the clipboard, where it remains until something new is copied or cut over it.

- To copy and save more than one selection, use the Spike feature (see **Spike**).

- To move information between applications use the **Embed** or **Link** feature.

Drag-and-Drop (Copy)

1   Click and drag over text or graphics to select for copying.

2   Press and hold the **Ctrl** key, then click and drag selected information to the new location (the insertion point will contain a gray square and a square with a plus sign (+) inside it to indicate that you are dragging a copy).

3   Release the mouse button at the spot where you want the copied information to appear.

Toolbar

1   Click and drag over text or graphics to select for copying.

2   Click the Copy button 🗐.

3   Point to and click the spot to paste copied information.

4   Click the Paste button 🗐.

Menu

1   Click and drag over text or graphics to select for copying.

2   Click **Edit**, **Copy**.

3   Point to and click the spot to paste copied information.

4   Click **Edit**, **Paste**.

Cut/Move Information

Use the Cut and Paste commands to move text, formatting and graphics and place them elsewhere in the document, or into a different document. Because it is such a common word processing task, there are several ways to cut and paste information.

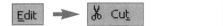 

Notes:

- The keyboard short-cut for cutting infor-mation is Ctrl + X.

- If drag-and-drop does not work, the drag-and-drop feature may not be turned on. To turn it on, click Tools, Options, select the Edit tab, and click the Drag-and-drop text editing option.

- Cut information is placed on the clipboard, where it remains until some-thing new is copied or cut over it.

- To cut and save more than one selection, use the Spike feature.

- You can move information from many (but not all) applications to Word.

- To move information between applications use the Embed or Link features.

Drag-and-drop (Move)

1 Click and drag over text or graphics to select for moving.

2 Click and drag highlighted information to the new location (the insertion point will contain a gray square to indicate that you are dragging information).

3 Release the mouse button at the spot where you want the information to appear.

Toolbar

1 Click and drag over text or graphics to select for moving.

2 Click the Cut button 🔏.

3 Point to and click the spot to paste cut information.

4 Click the Paste button 📋.

Menu

1 Click and drag over text or graphics to select for moving.

2 Click **Edit**, **Cut**.

3 Point to and click the spot to paste cut information.

4 Click **Edit**, **Paste**.

Find Text

The Find command searches for matching information or formatting throughout a document.

Notes:

- The keyboard short-cut to begin a text search is Ctrl + F.

- Wildcards can help make your searches more flexible. In the Find what box, use an asterisk (*) to represent any number of characters, a question mark (?) to represent any character, a dollar sign ($) to represent any letter and a pound sign (#) to represent any digit.

- You can copy and paste any character from your document to the Find what box.

1 Click **Edit**, **Find** to open the Find dialog box.

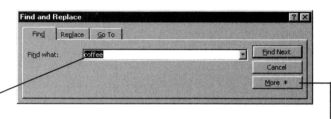

2 Type the information to be searched for in the **Find what** text box
OR
Click the **Find what** drop-down button to choose from pasted items.

3 To display advanced find features, click the **More** button.

4 Click the **Search** drop-down button to change the direction of the search.

5 Click the checkbox of any additional Search option to further specify the type of search:
- **Match case** to find only the text with the same capitalization as the Find what text.
- **Find whole words only** to limit the found text to exactly the words specified, and not the Find what text embedded within larger words.
- **Use wildcards** to treat * and ? as wildcards and not literal text.
- **Sounds like** to search text phonetically.
- **Find all word forms** to find other forms of the same word.

6 Click the **Format** drop-down button to include

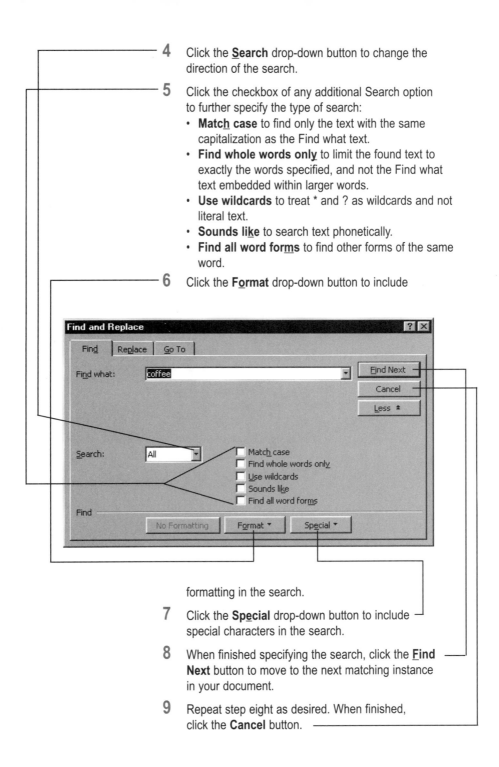

formatting in the search.

7 Click the **Special** drop-down button to include special characters in the search.

8 When finished specifying the search, click the **Find Next** button to move to the next matching instance in your document.

9 Repeat step eight as desired. When finished, click the **Cancel** button.

Go To

Quickly go to a page, bookmark, line or other document landmark. (See also **Move Around within a Document**).

Notes:

- The Go To feature is especially helpful when working with long documents. It enables you to search quickly through your document and locate specific information.

1   Click **Edit**, **Go To** to open the Find and Replace dialog box.

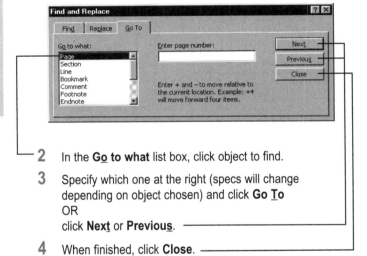

2   In the **Go to what** list box, click object to find.

3   Specify which one at the right (specs will change depending on object chosen) and click **Go To**
OR
click **Next** or **Previous**. ───────────

4   When finished, click **Close**. ───────────

Continue

⟶

Grammar

The grammar checker analyzes your text and uses a wavy green underline to point out what might be trouble spots. The grammar checker can be customized to suit the type of writing that is being checked: formal, informal, technical or other.

1 Right-click an area of text with a wavy green underline.

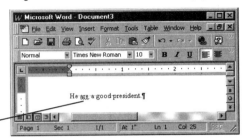

2 Click a boldface suggestion to replace the text
OR
click **Grammar** to display the Grammar dialog box.

- Click a **Suggestion**, then click the **Change** button.
- Click **Ignore** to go to the next grammatical error.
- Click **Ignore All** to ignore identical instances.

Customize Grammar Checking

1   Click **Tools**, **Options** to display the Spelling & Grammar
    options dialog box
    OR
    in the Grammar dialog box, click the **Options** button.

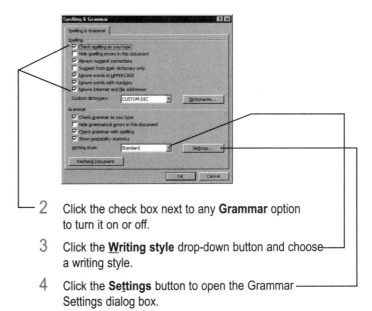

2   Click the check box next to any **Grammar** option
    to turn it on or off.

3   Click the **Writing style** drop-down button and choose
    a writing style.

4   Click the **Settings** button to open the Grammar
    Settings dialog box.

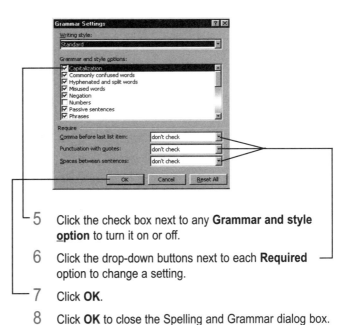

5   Click the check box next to any **Grammar and style
    option** to turn it on or off.

6   Click the drop-down buttons next to each **Required**
    option to change a setting.

7   Click **OK**.

8   Click **OK** to close the Spelling and Grammar dialog box.

Hyphenation

Word can be set to automatically hyphenate words in your document to make the right edge less jagged. There are also several types of hyphens that can be used to separate words.

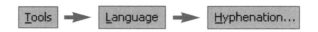

Notes:

- To keep Word from automatically hyphenating selected text, click Don't hyphenate on the Line and Page Breaks tab of the Paragraph dialog box (see **Format Paragraph**).

- To hyphenate selected text manually, open the Hyphenation dialog and click the Manual button.

- Use the Non-breaking Hyphen feature to assure that a particular word always remains unbroken on a line. Highlight the word and press Ctrl+Shift+Hyphen.

- Use the Optional Hyphen feature when a word only needs to be broken at the end of a line. Highlight the word and press Ctrl+Hyphen.

Automatic Hyphenation

1 Click **Tools**, **Language**, **Hyphenation** to open the Hyphenation dialog box.

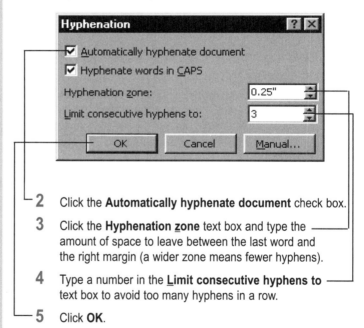

2 Click the **Automatically hyphenate document** check box.

3 Click the **Hyphenation zone** text box and type the amount of space to leave between the last word and the right margin (a wider zone means fewer hyphens).

4 Type a number in the **Limit consecutive hyphens to** text box to avoid too many hyphens in a row.

5 Click **OK**.

Insert File

The Insert File command inserts the entire contents of another file into the current document.

Notes:

- To insert only part of a file, type a bookmark name in the Range box.

1 Click desired location to insert file contents.

2 Click **Insert**, **File** to open the Insert File dialog box.

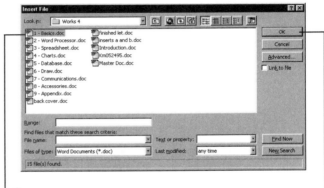

3 Select or type desired filename to insert (see **Open Document** and **Files and Folders**).

4 Click **OK**.

115

Master Document

The Master Document feature can be used to organize multiple documents into one larger document.

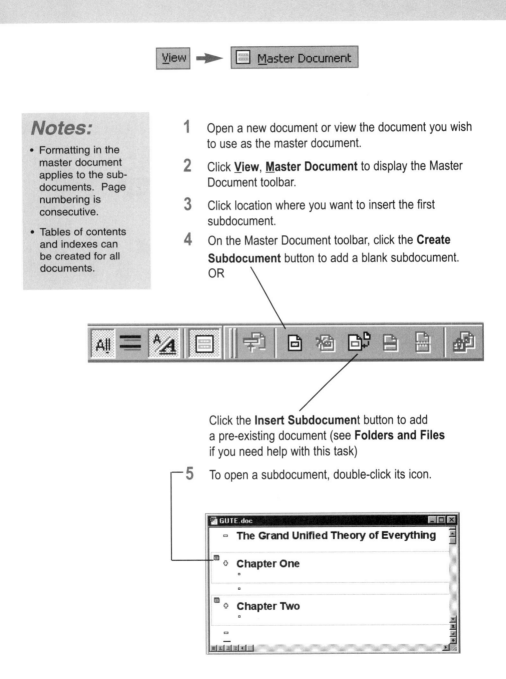

View ➡ 🔲 Master Document

Notes:

- Formatting in the master document applies to the sub-documents. Page numbering is consecutive.

- Tables of contents and indexes can be created for all documents.

1 Open a new document or view the document you wish to use as the master document.

2 Click **View**, **Master Document** to display the Master Document toolbar.

3 Click location where you want to insert the first subdocument.

4 On the Master Document toolbar, click the **Create Subdocument** button to add a blank subdocument.
OR

Click the **Insert Subdocument** button to add a pre-existing document (see **Folders and Files** if you need help with this task)

5 To open a subdocument, double-click its icon.

GUTE.doc

 ▫ **The Grand Unified Theory of Everything**

 ⬦ **Chapter One**

 ⬦ **Chapter Two**

Expand or Collapse Subdocuments

1   To expand all subdocuments, click the Expand

    Subdocuments button 🖽.

2   To collapse all subdocuments, click the Collapse

    Subdocuments button 🖅.

Move a Subdocument

1   Click a subdocument's icon to select it.

2   Click and drag the subdocument to the new location.

Remove Subdocuments

1   Expand subdocuments (see above).

2   Click the subdocument to remove

    and then click the subdocument button 🗏.

Merge Subdocuments

1   Expand the master document.

2   Move the subdocuments to be combined next to each
    other.

3   Click the icon for the first document to select it. Hold the
    Shift key and click the icons for the remaining documents.

4   Click the Merge Documents button 🖹.

Split Subdocuments

1   Expand the master document.

2   Select or create a heading in the subdocument to use as a
    new subdocument heading (see **Outline** to create a head-
    ing).

3   Click the Split Documents button 🖹.

Replace Text

The Replace command allows you to search for information or formatting in a document and replace it with text or formatting that you specify.

1 Click **Edit**, **Replace** to open the Find and Replace dialog box.

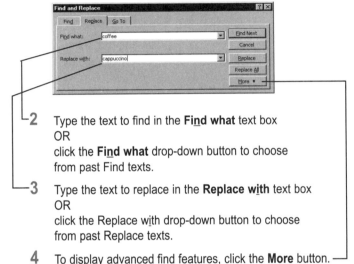

2 Type the text to find in the **Find what** text box
OR
click the **Find what** drop-down button to choose from past Find texts.

3 Type the text to replace in the **Replace with** text box
OR
click the Replace with drop-down button to choose from past Replace texts.

4 To display advanced find features, click the **More** button.

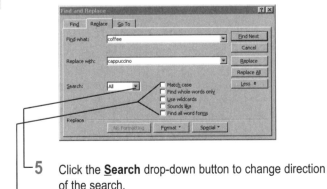

5 Click the **Search** drop-down button to change direction of the search.

6 Click the checkbox of any additional Search option to further specify the type of search:
- **Match case** to find only the text with the same capitalization as the *Find what* text.

118

- **Find whole words only** to limit the found text to exactly the words specified, and not the Find what text embedded within larger words.
- **Use wildcards** to treat * and ? as wildcards and not literal text.
- **Sounds like** to search text phonetically.
- **Find all word forms** to find other forms of the same word.

7 Click the **Format** drop-down button to include formatting in the Find what or Replace with text.

8 Click the **Special** drop-down button to include special characters in the Find what or Replace with text.

9 When finished specifying the search, click the **Find Next** button to move to the next matching instance in your document.

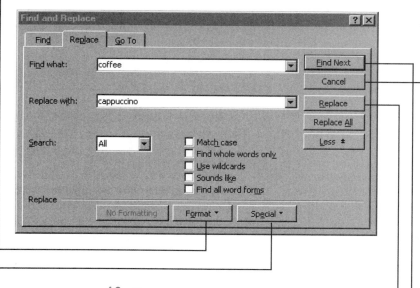

10 Click the **Replace** button to replace the found text with the Replace with text
OR
click **Find Next** button to leave the found text as is and find the next matching text.

11 Repeat step ten as desired
OR
click **Replace All** to automatically replace all instances of matching text with replacement text.

12 When finished, click **Cancel**.

119

Spelling

Word automatically checks the spelling of the words in your document and underlines those it does not recognize with a wavy red line.

Tools ➡ ABC Spelling and Grammar...

Notes:

- The keyboard short-cut for activating a spelling check is F7.

- The wavy red under-line under misspelled words does not print.

- Clear the Check grammar checkbox in the Spelling dialog box to avoid a grammar check.

1 Right-click the misspelled word.

2 From the list of possible spelling choices, click desired spelling
OR
click **Ignore All** to accept the word throughout the document
OR
click **Add** to add the word to Word's dictionary. This will prevent the word from being specified as misspelled in all future documents.

Toolbar

Click the spelling button ABC to bring up the Spelling and Grammar dialog box.

Dialog box

1 Click **Tools**, **Spelling and Grammar** to open the Spelling dialog box
OR
click the Spelling button.

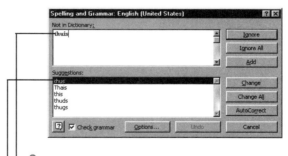

2 The first misspelled word will appear in the
Not in Dictionary text box. You can do one of the following:
- Click the correctly spelled word in the **Suggestions** list and click **Change**.
- Click the correctly spelled word in the Suggestions list and click **Change All** to correct all identical misspellings throughout the document.

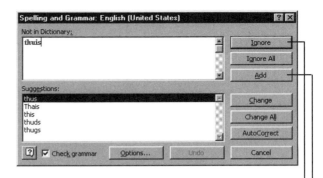

- Click the correctly spelled word in the **Suggestions** list and click **AutoCorrect** to automatically correct the identical misspelling when you type it in the future.
- Click **Ignore** to leave the word as it is and go on to the next word.
- Click **Add** to add the word to the dictionary for future spell checks.

3 Repeat step 2 until all words are checked.

4 Click **OK** to close the Spelling and Grammar dialog box.

Sort a List

Word can sort many kinds of lists alphabetically or numerically.

Notes:

- To sort a list in a table see **Tables: Sort Cell Contents**.

- To avoid including list titles or headers in your sort, click the Header row button in the Sort Text dialog box.

- When sorting text, Word puts punctuation marks first, numbers next, then letters.

- When sorting numbers, Word ignores all text and punctuation. The number can be anywhere in the paragraph.

* Word recognizes slashes (/), commas and periods as valid

1 Click and drag to select text to sort.

2 Click **Table**, **Sort** to open the Sort Text dialog box.

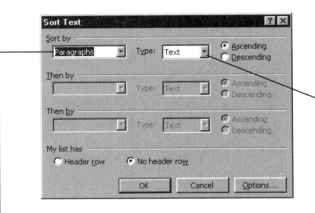

3 Click **Sort by** drop-down button to choose the first sort priority (Your choices will vary depending on the text you selected):
- **Paragraphs** sorts by the characters following a line return.
- **Field 1** also sorts by the characters following a line return.
- **Field 2** sorts by the characters following a tab.

4 Click the **Type** drop-down button to choose an information type:
- **Text** to sort information containing both text and numbers (numbers will be sorted as if they were text).
- **Number** to sort numbers by their actual value.
- **Date** to sort dates typed in any regular format.

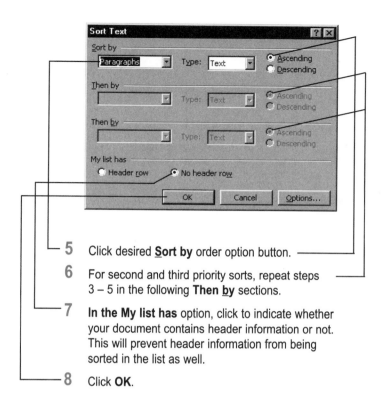

5 Click desired **Sort by** order option button.

6 For second and third priority sorts, repeat steps 3 – 5 in the following **Then by** sections.

7 **In the My list has** option, click to indicate whether your document contains header information or not. This will prevent header information from being sorted in the list as well.

8 Click **OK**.

123

Spike

Use the Spike feature to save various nonadjacent text selections and then be able to paste them as a group to a new location or document.

Create a Spike

1 Click and drag to select text or graphics to move to the Spike.

2 Press Ctrl + F3.

3 Repeat for each selection you wish to add to the spike.

Insert a Spike

1 Click location to place the Spike's contents.

2 Press Ctrl + Shift + F3.

View Spike Contents

1   Click **Insert**, **AutoText**, **AutoText** to open the AutoCorrect
    dialog box.Be sure the **AutoText** tab is selected.

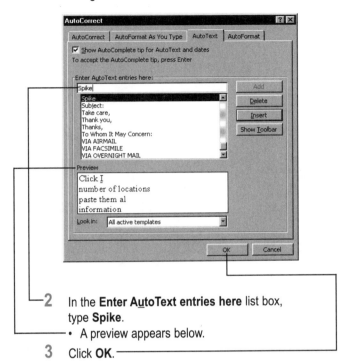

2   In the **Enter AutoText entries here** list box,
    type **Spike**.
    • A preview appears below.

3   Click **OK**.

Thesaurus

The Thesaurus is used to find words that have similar meanings.

Notes:

- The keyboard shortcut for accessing the thesaurus is Shift + F7.

- The Looked Up drop-down list contains a running list of all the words whose meanings you have explored. Click the drop-down arrow to return to one of your previous choices.

1 Click word to look up.

2 Click **Tools**, **Language**, **Thesaurus** to open the Thesaurus dialog box.

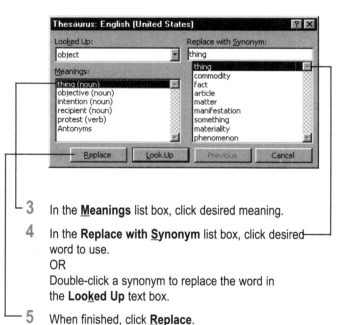

3 In the **Meanings** list box, click desired meaning.

4 In the **Replace with Synonym** list box, click desired word to use.
OR
Double-click a synonym to replace the word in the **Looked Up** text box.

5 When finished, click **Replace**.

126

Continue

Track Changes

Word can track changes to a document and indicate those changes in a different color or text style. The changes can then be accepted or rejected.

Notes:

- You can use the scroll bar to browse a document by edits (see **Move Around within a Document**).

- Change the name or initials used in comments on the User Information tab of the Options dialog box (see **Options**).

1 Click **Tools**, **Track Changes**, **Highlight Changes** to open the Highlight Changes dialog box.

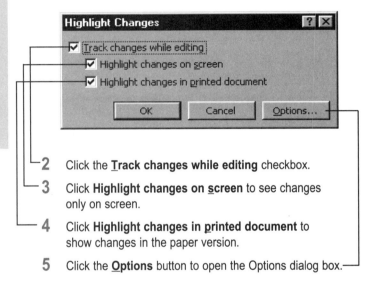

2 Click the **Track changes while editing** checkbox.

3 Click **Highlight changes on screen** to see changes only on screen.

4 Click **Highlight changes in printed document** to show changes in the paper version.

5 Click the **Options** button to open the Options dialog box.

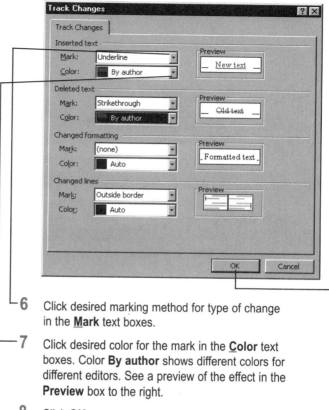

6 Click desired marking method for type of change in the **Mark** text boxes.

7 Click desired color for the mark in the **Color** text boxes. Color **By author** shows different colors for different editors. See a preview of the effect in the **Preview** box to the right.

8 Click **OK**.

9 Edit document as desired.

Review Changes

1 Right-click on any toolbar and click **Reviewing** to display the Reviewing toolbar.

2 Click Next Change button [image] or Previous Change button [image] to move from change to change.

3 Click Accept Change button [image] to remove highlighting and change the text
OR

Click Reject Change button [image] to revert to the original text.

Word Count

Counts the number of words, lines and paragraphs in the current document.

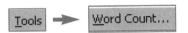

1 Click **Tools**, **Word Count** to open the Word Count dialog box.

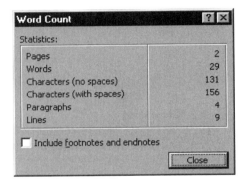

2 Click **Close**.

Tables

Word can present information in attractively
formatted tables within your documents.
In this section you will learn to create, edit
and format tables, as well as how to sort
table contents.

Tables: Create a Table

Tables are useful to arrange text or numbers in column or row format. Tables can be formatted with a variety of border and shading styles.

Notes:

- To create newspaper style columns, use the Columns feature (see **Columns**).

- To include a section of an Excel spreadsheet in your document see **Embed** or **Link**.

Create a Simple Table

1 On the Standard toolbar, click the Insert Table button [image] and drag over desired number of columns and rows (you can also add and remove columns and rows later).

2 Click **Table**, **Table AutoFormat** to open the AutoFormat dialog box.

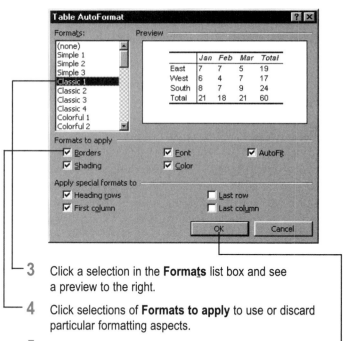

3 Click a selection in the **Formats** list box and see a preview to the right.

4 Click selections of **Formats to apply** to use or discard particular formatting aspects.

5 Click **OK**. ——————————————

6 To add information to the table, point and click the first cell.

7 Type information, then press **Tab** to move to next cell.

Create a Complicated or Irregular Table

1 On the standard toolbar, click the Tables and Borders

button 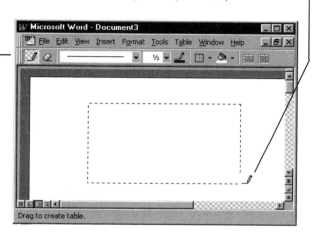. The **Tables and Borders** toolbar appears and the insertion point changes to a pencil shape.

2 Click and drag to draw a rectangle the size of the entire table.

3 Click and drag to draw columns and rows inside the table.

4 To erase a line, click the Eraser button and drag over line to remove.

5 To add more lines, click the Draw Table button.

6 To add information to the table, point and click first cell.

7 Type information, then press **Tab** to move to next cell.

Tables: Edit a Table

You can add or remove rows and columns from a table at any time.

Notes:

- To apply formats or edits to a whole table, click Table, Select Table.

- To display the Table and Borders toolbar, right-click any toolbar and click Tables and Borders.

Insert a Column

1 Point to and click the area just above the table where you want to add the columns.

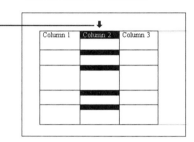

2 Click the Insert Columns button. (The button becomes visible once the column is selected.) The original columns will shift to the right to accommodate the new column.

Insert Row

1 Point to and click or click and drag in the area just left of the table where you want to add the rows.

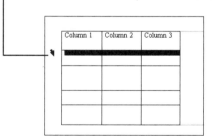

2 Click the Insert Rows button. (The button becomes visible once the column is selected.) The original rows will shift down to accommodate the new row.

Remove Rows or Columns

1 Click and drag area to left of rows or above columns to remove.

2 Click **Table**, **Delete Rows** or **Delete Columns**.

Split Cells

1 Click and drag to select cells to split.

2 On the Tables and Borders toolbar, click the Split Cells

button 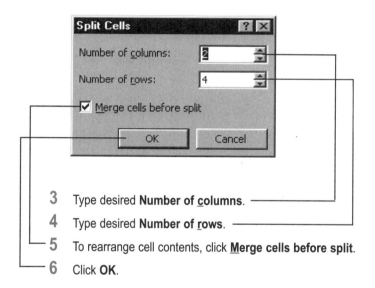 to open the Split Cells dialog box
OR
click **Table**, **Split Cells**.

3 Type desired **Number of columns**. ——————————

4 Type desired **Number of rows**. ——————————

5 To rearrange cell contents, click **Merge cells before split**.

6 Click **OK**.

Merge Cells

1 Click and drag over cells to merge.

2 On the Tables and Borders toolbar, click the Merge

Cells button
OR
Click **Table**, **Merge Cells**.

135

Tables: Format a Table

Tables can be made more informative and attractive with the addition of borders, shading and other graphical formatting.

Notes:

- To apply formats or edits to a whole table, click Table, Select Table.

- To display the Table and Borders toolbar, right-click any toolbar and click Tables and Borders.

Text Align

1 Click and drag over cells to align.

2 Click desired alignment button on the Standard toolbar:

- **Left align**

- **Right align**

- **Justify** (both left and right align)

- **Center align**.

Format Font

1 Click and drag over cells to change.

2 To change the typeface, click the **Font** drop-down button

Times New Roman ▼ on the Formatting toolbar and click desired font.

3 To change font size, click the **Font Size** drop-down button

10 ▼ and click desired size.

4 To make font bold, click the Bold button **B**.

5 To make font italicized, click the Italics button *I*.

6 To underline text, click the Underline button U.

7 To change text color, click the **Font Color** drop-down button A ▼.

Change Borders and Shading

1 Click and drag over cells to change.

2 On the Tables and Borders toolbar, click the Line Style button [_____ ▼] and select style to use.

3 Click the Line Weight drop-down button [½ ▼] and select desired line width.

4 Click the Border Color button [✎] and select line color.

5 Click the Borders button [▦ ▼] and select which edges to border.

6 Click the Shading Color button [▨ ▼] and select color or shading to fill cells.

Change Cell Margins

Note: The text or number margins in the cells are changed by moving the indent markers.

1 If necessary, click **View**, **Ruler** to display the rulers.

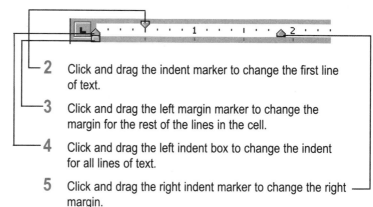

2 Click and drag the indent marker to change the first line of text.

3 Click and drag the left margin marker to change the margin for the rest of the lines in the cell.

4 Click and drag the left indent box to change the indent for all lines of text.

5 Click and drag the right indent marker to change the right margin.

Add Table Numbers

Word can automatically add numbers in a table.

1 Click cell at end of column or row of numbers.

2 On the Tables and Borders toolbar, click the

137

Tables: Sort Cell Contents

Information in columns, whether text or numbers, can be sorted automatically.

1 If desired, select single column to sort by.

2 Click **Table**, **Sort** to open the Sort dialog box.

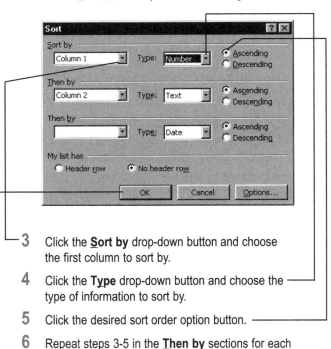

3 Click the **Sort by** drop-down button and choose the first column to sort by.

4 Click the **Type** drop-down button and choose the type of information to sort by.

5 Click the desired sort order option button.

6 Repeat steps 3-5 in the **Then by** sections for each additional priority column.

7 Click **OK**.

Sort by Selected Column

1   Point to and click above column to sort by.

2   Click **Table**, **Sort** to open the Sort dialog box.

3   Click **Options** to open the Options dialog box.

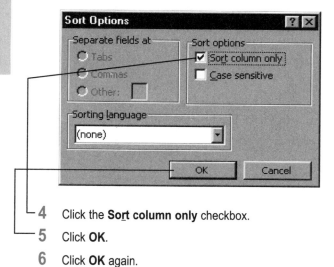

4   Click the **Sort column only** checkbox.

5   Click **OK**.

6   Click **OK** again.

Graphics

This section will introduce you to some of Word's extensive graphic capabilities You will learn how to insert pictures and clip art into your documents as well as how to arrange text around or through pictures or text. You will learn to create borders, shading, and text boxes. This chapter also covers Word's WordArt feature, which enables you to graphically alter your text.

AutoShapes

AutoShapes is a collection of shapes and drawings–such as banners, arrows and callouts–which can be inserted into documents and customized.

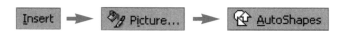

Notes:

- Add colors, shadows and 3-D effects to the AutoShape by using the Drawing toolbar.
- To display the Drawing toolbar, right click on any toolbar and click Drawing.

1 Click **Insert**, **Picture**, **AutoShapes** to display the AutoShapes and Drawing toolbars.

2 Click desired shape to draw, then choose a specific shape:

- Lines
- Basic Shapes
- Block Arrows
- Flowchart
- Stars and Banners
- Callouts

3 Click and drag on document page to draw the AutoShape (for curvy lines, double-click when finished).

4 To make shape smaller or larger, click and drag a handle.

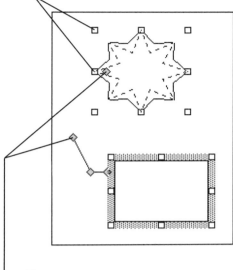

5 Many shapes have a diamond handle to click and drag to change specific proportions of the AutoShape (to make stars pointier, for instance, or to change the stem of a callout).

6 Return to the document window by clicking outside the AutoShape.

Borders: Create Borders for Pages

Your pages can be bordered by a variety of lines, colors and shapes.

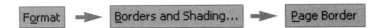

Notes:

- To change each border separately, click desired line style and—in the Preview area—click the border to change.

1   Click **Format**, **Borders and Shading** to open the Borders and Shading dialog box.

2   Click the **Page Border** tab to bring it to the front.

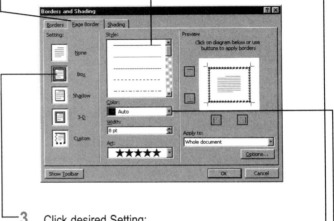

3   Click desired Setting:
- **None** to remove a border
- **Box** for a border that is the same on all sides
- **Shadow** for a shadowed effect
- **3-D** for a three dimensional effect
- **Custom** to choose different borders for different sides.

4   In the **Style** list box, click desired border style (check the Preview to the right to see the effect you've created).

5   Click the **Color** drop-down button to choose a color for the border.

144

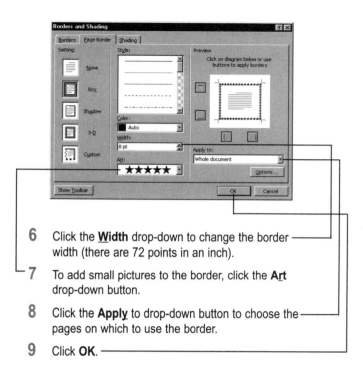

6 Click the **Width** drop-down to change the border width (there are 72 points in an inch).

7 To add small pictures to the border, click the **Art** drop-down button.

8 Click the **Apply** to drop-down button to choose the pages on which to use the border.

9 Click **OK**.

Borders: Create Borders for Paragraphs

Paragraphs can be bordered and shaded by a variety of lines and colors. You can add borders by using toolbar buttons. Additional border options are available within the Borders and Shading dialog box.

Notes:

- To change each border separately, click desired line style and – in the Preview area – click the border to change.

Toolbar

1 If necessary, right-click on any toolbar area and click Tables and Borders to display the toolbar.

2 Click and drag over text to border.

3 Click the Line Style drop-down button

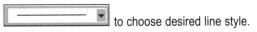 to choose desired line style.

4 Click the Line Weight drop-down button to choose desired line weight.

5 Click the Border Color button to click desired line color.

6 Click the Borders drop-down button to choose which sides to border.

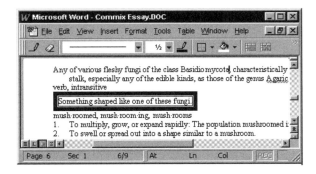

Dialog Box

1   Click **Format**, **Borders and Shading** to open the Borders and Shading dialog box.

2   Click the **Borders** tab to bring it to the front.

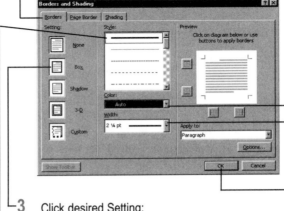

3   Click desired Setting:
   - **None** to remove a border
   - **Box** for a border that is the same on all sides
   - **Shadow** for a shadowed effect
   - **3-D** for a three dimensional effect
   - **Custom** to choose different borders for different sides.

4   In the **Style** list box, click desired border style (check the Preview to the right to see the effect you've created).

5   Click the **Color** drop-down button to choose a color ─── for the border.

6   Click the **Width** drop-down to change the border ──────── width (there are 72 points in an inch).

7   Click **OK**.─────────────────────────────────────

Drawing

The Drawing feature allows you to create your own drawing or edit a pre-existing drawing.

Notes:

- Drawing features can be used to format clip art, text boxes, WordArt and AutoShapes.

Create a Shape

1   On the Standard toolbar, click the Drawing button to display the Drawing toolbar.

2   Click desired toolbar button:

- Line button
- Arrow button
- Rectangle button
- Oval button

3   Click and drag to create the desired shape.

Change the Size of a Drawing

1   Click the drawing object to be changed. To select additional objects to edit at the same time, hold the Shift key and click each additional object. Each object will be surrounded by four to eight squares. These squares are referred to as handles.

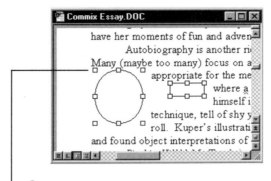

2   To change the size of selected objects, point to a handle (the pointer will appear as a two-headed arrow) and drag the handle out or in.

Move a Drawing

1   Click the drawing object to be moved. To select additional objects to move at the same time, hold the Shift key and click each additional object.

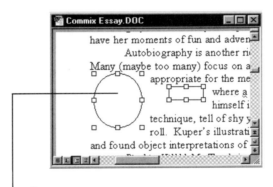

2   To move selected objects, point to an area within the area surrounded by the handles (the pointer will appear as a four-headed arrow), then click and drag the objects to the desired new location.

Change Appearance of Drawing

*Note: Outline, fill, and other aspects can be changed
depending on the type of drawing you are
editing.*

1   On the Standard toolbar, click the Drawing button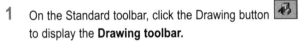
to display the **Drawing toolbar.**

2   Click the drawing object to be changed. To select additional
objects to edit at the same time, hold the Shift key and click
each additional object.

3   Click the following toolbar buttons to use access certain
effects:

- **Fill Color** drop-down button ⬛ to change the interi-
or color of the drawing.

- **Line Color** drop-down button ⬛ to change the color
of the outline.

- **Font Color** drop-down button ⬛ to change the color
of interior text.

- **Line Style** drop-down ⬛ to change the width and
style of outline.

- **Dash Style** drop-down ⬛ to choose a dashed outline.

- **Shadow** drop-down ⬛ to choose a shadow.

- **3-D** drop-down ⬛ to choose a three-dimensional
effect.

Rotate Drawing

1   On the standard toolbar, click the Drawing button
    to display the **Drawing toolbar.**

2   Click drawing object to rotate. To select additional objects
    to rotate at the same time, hold the Shift key and click
    each additional object.

3   Click the Free Rotate button ⟨icon⟩. The handles at the
    corners become circles and the pointer changes to a rota-
    tion symbol.

4   Click and drag a handle until drawing is rotated as desired.

Flip Drawing

1   On the standard toolbar, click the Drawing button ⟨icon⟩
    to display the **Drawing toolbar.**

2   Click drawing object to change. To select additional objects
    to edit at the same time, hold the **Shift** key and click each
    additional object.

3   Click the Draw drop-down button 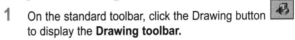.

4   Click **Rotate** or **Flip,** then click desired new position.

151

Group Drawings

Several drawing objects can be combined into one object to make editing easier.

1 On the Standard toolbar, click the Drawing button to display the **Drawing toolbar.**

2 Click first drawing object. To select additional objects, hold the Shift key and click each additional object.

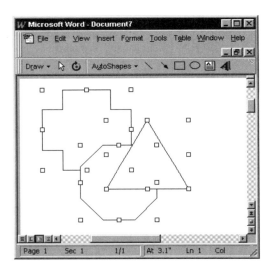

3 Click the Draw drop-down button Draw ▾
OR
right-click the shapes and click **Grouping**.

4 Click **Group**. The objects will have only one set of handles.

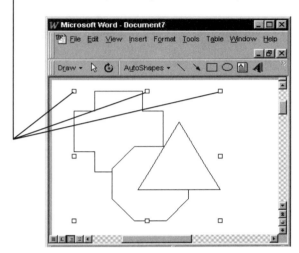

Change Object Overlap

1 On the Standard toolbar, click the Drawing button
to display the **Drawing toolbar**.

2 Click first object.

3 Click the Draw drop-down button Draw ▾
OR
right-click object.

4 Click **Order**, then click desired position of object.

Pictures: Insert and Edit Clip Art and Pictures

There are many ways of including images in your documents.
(See also Drawing and AutoShape)

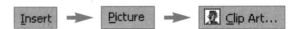

Insert → Picture → 📇 Clip Art...

Notes:

- Click the Import Clips button in the Clip Art Gallery window to add clip art to the gallery.

- Click the Find button in the Clip Gallery window to search for the art based on key words.

- Click the Pictures, Sounds or Videos tabs to add other types of clips to your documents.

Insert Clip Art

Insert an image from Word's clip art collection, or from a clip art collection of your own.

1 Click **Insert**, **Picture**, **Clip Art** to open the Clip Gallery window.

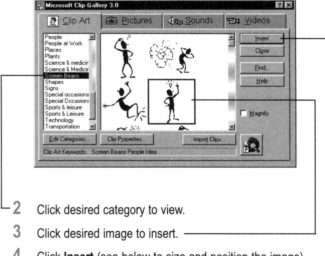

2 Click desired category to view.

3 Click desired image to insert. ⎯⎯⎯⎯⎯

4 Click **Insert** (see below to size and position the image).⎯⎯

Insert Picture

Inserts an image saved to a separate file.

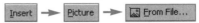

1 Click **Insert**, **Picture**, **From File** to open the Insert Picture dialog box.

2 Select desired file name (see **Folders and Files** if you need help with this step).

3 Click **Insert** (see below to size and position the image).

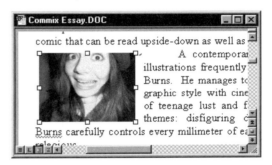

Change Image Size

1 If necessary, click picture to select it.

2 Click and drag one of the picture's handles to the desired size

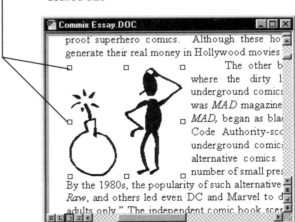

Pictures: Text Wrap Around Images

Text can be unwrapped around an image for decorative display. See also **Text Boxes**.

Notes:

- Text may be wrapped around clip-art, scanned art, illustrations, monograms or any other object to create a decorative effect.

Alter Text Wrapping

1   If necessary, click text box to select it.

2   Click **Format**, **Picture**
OR
right-click the text box, click **Format Picture**.

3   Click the **Wrapping** tab.

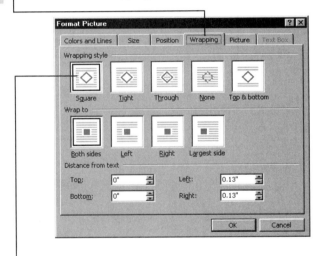

4   Click a **Wrapping style** to change the way text flows around the picture:
- **Square** to wrap text around the picture
- **Tight** to push text to the very edges of the drawing itself
- **Through** to run text between drawing lines
- **None** to run text through the text box
- **Top & bottom** to leave areas to the left and right of the text box blank.

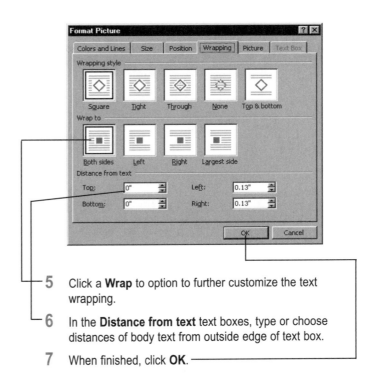

5 Click a **Wrap** to option to further customize the text wrapping.

6 In the **Distance from text** text boxes, type or choose distances of body text from outside edge of text box.

7 When finished, click **OK**.

Text Boxes

The Text Box feature is used to format quotes, side bars and other text within an outlined or shaded box. The text box itself can be surrounded by thick or thin lines. It can also be shadowed, shaded or colored.

Notes:

- To add a colored block behind a paragraph, you can also use Text Shading.

- To keep a text box with a specific paragraph, use the Move object with text and the Lock anchor checkboxes on the Position tab of the Format Text Box dialog.

Create a Text Box

1   Click **Insert**, **Text box**. The pointer turns into a large plus sign.

2   Click and drag to draw a text box of a desired size.

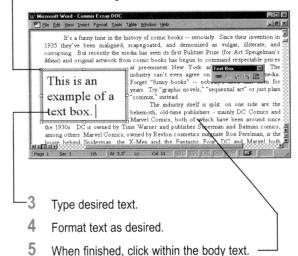

3   Type desired text.

4   Format text as desired.

5   When finished, click within the body text.

Format a Text Box

1   If necessary, click text box to select it.

2   Click **Format**
    OR
    Right-click the text box.

3   Click **Format Text Box** to open the Format Text Box dialog box.

158

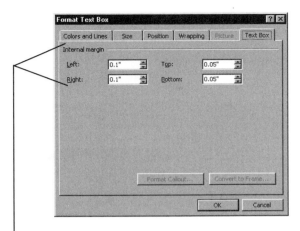

4 Type desired internal margins (the distance of the text inside the box to the box border) in the **Left**, **Right**, **Top** and **Bottom** text boxes.

5 To change text box borders, click the **Colors and Lines** tab.

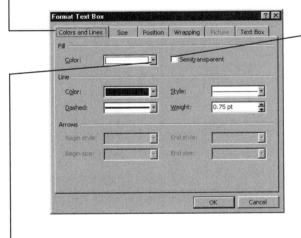

6 Click the **Fill Color** drop-down arrow to change the color inside the text box.

7 Click the **Semitransparent** checkbox to lighten the chosen color.

159

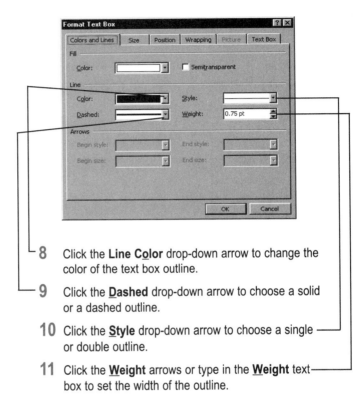

8 Click the **Line Color** drop-down arrow to change the color of the text box outline.

9 Click the **Dashed** drop-down arrow to choose a solid or a dashed outline.

10 Click the **Style** drop-down arrow to choose a single or double outline.

11 Click the **Weight** arrows or type in the **Weight** text box to set the width of the outline.

12 Click the Wrapping tab to change the text wrapping

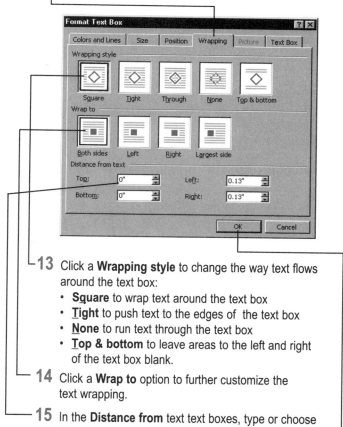

13 Click a **Wrapping style** to change the way text flows around the text box:
- **Square** to wrap text around the text box
- **Tight** to push text to the edges of the text box
- **None** to run text through the text box
- **Top & bottom** to leave areas to the left and right of the text box blank.

14 Click a **Wrap to** option to further customize the text wrapping.

15 In the **Distance from** text text boxes, type or choose distances of body text from outside edge of text box.

16 When finished, click **OK**.

Text Boxes *continued . . .*

Notes:

* Surrounding text can be set to flow around or through a text box in a variety of ways.

Change Text Box Size

1 Click desired text box to select it.

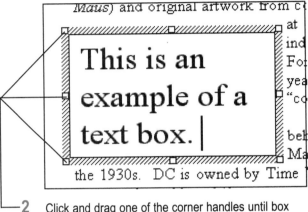

2 Click and drag one of the corner handles until box reaches desired size.

Link Text Boxes

Linked Text boxes allow you to flow text from one box to the next. If text is edited or box size is changed, text automatically flows between boxes to fill the space.

1 Create two or more empty text boxes (see above).

2 Click the first text box to select it.

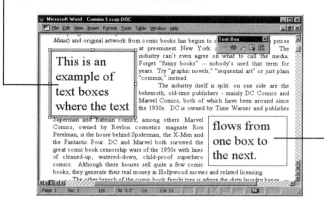

3 On the Text Box toolbar, click the Create Text Box Link button ![icon] (the pointer changes to a pitcher).

4 Click the following text box (the pitcher pours).

5 Repeat steps 2-4 for each link.

Break Links Between Text Boxes

1 Click first box containing link to break.

2 Click the Break Forward Link button ![icon]

Text Shading

A colored background can be added to text for emphasis. Use the Tables and Borders toolbar or the Borders and Shadings dialog box.

Notes:

- To change the color of the text, select the text and click the Font Color drop-down button 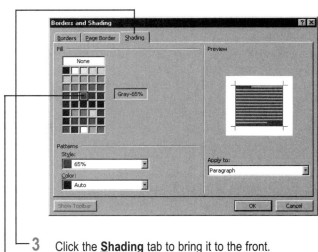 on the Formatting toolbar to select a different color.

- Right click on any selected text to access more Font formatting options.

Toolbar

1 If necessary, right-click on any toolbar and click **Tables and Borders** to display the toolbar.

2 Click and drag over text to shade.

3 Click the **Shading Color** drop-down button to choose shading color.

Dialog Box

1 Click and drag over text to shade.

2 Click **Format**, **Borders and Shading** to open the Borders and Shading dialog box.

3 Click the **Shading** tab to bring it to the front.

4 Click desired **Fill** color.

164

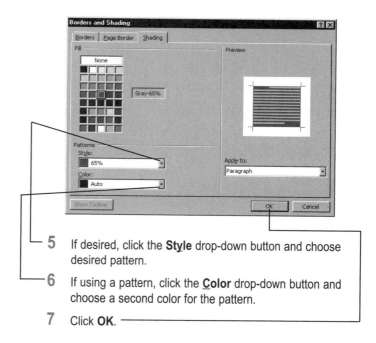

5 If desired, click the **Style** drop-down button and choose desired pattern.

6 If using a pattern, click the **Color** drop-down button and choose a second color for the pattern.

7 Click **OK**.

Watermark: Insert a Watermark on a Page

A word processing watermark is a lightly shaded image that appears behind text on a page.

Place Image as Background

1 Insert a picture onto a page (see also Pictures).

2 Click on image to select it.

3 Size and position image as desired.

4 Click **Format, Picture** and select the **Picture** tab in the Format Picture dialog box.

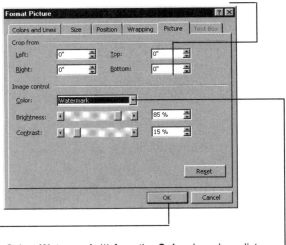

5 Select **Watermark** (*) from the **Color** drop-down list.

6 Click **OK**.

Place a Transparent Text Box over a Watermark Image

1   Click the Textbox button ▣ on the Drawing toolbar.

2   Click and drag to draw a textbox over the Watermark image.

3   Type the desired text in the text box.

4   Select the textbox and click the Fill Color drop-down

button ▣ ▾ on the Drawing toolbar, and select

| No Fill |

5   Click the Line Color drop-down button ▣ ▾ on the

Drawing toolbar, and select | No Line |

Watermark: Insert a Watermark as a Header or Footer

Inserting a watermark in the header or footer area assures that the image will be captured throughout the document

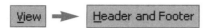

Notes:

- The watermark will be visible only in Page Layout view or Print Preview.

1 Click **View**, **Header and Footer** to display the header and footer areas.

2 Insert desired image in the header (see also **Picture**, **AutoShape**, **WordArt** and **Drawing**).

3 Size and position the image as desired.

4 Right-click the image and choose **Format Picture** from the shortcut menu to open the Format dialog box. Click the **Wrapping** tab.

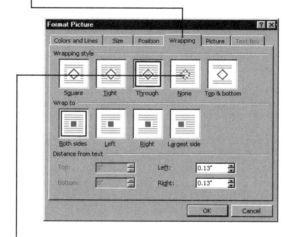

5 Click **None** as a Wrapping style. Click the **Picture** tab, if it is available.

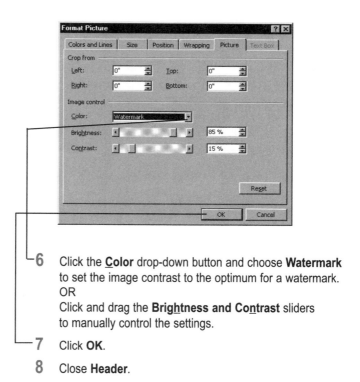

6 Click the **Color** drop-down button and choose **Watermark** to set the image contrast to the optimum for a watermark. OR

Click and drag the **Brightness and Contrast** sliders to manually control the settings.

7 Click **OK**.

8 Close **Header**.

WordArt

WordArt creates text that bends and twists and is dramatically colored, patterned and shadowed.

Notes:

- Many of the formatting effects used for drawings and text boxes can be used with WordArt (see also **Drawing** and **Text Boxes**).

1 On the standard toolbar, click the Drawing button to display the Drawing toolbar.

2 On the Drawing toolbar, click the WordArt button to display the WordArt Gallery dialog box.

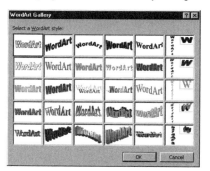

3 Click the style that best suits your need (you can change it later).

4 Click **OK** to open the Edit WordArt dialog box.

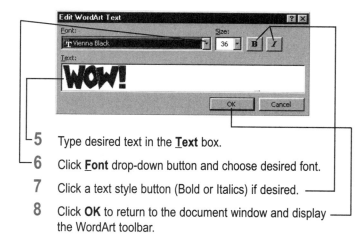

5 Type desired text in the **Text** box.

6 Click **Font** drop-down button and choose desired font.

7 Click a text style button (Bold or Italics) if desired. ——

8 Click **OK** to return to the document window and display —— the WordArt toolbar.

9 Click and drag a handle to make text larger or smaller.

10 Click and drag the diamond handle to exaggerate or reduce the shape proportions

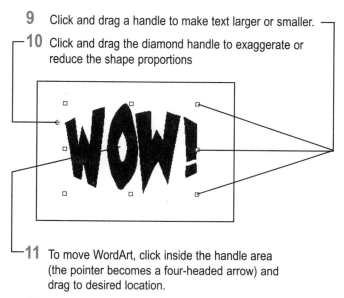

11 To move WordArt, click inside the handle area (the pointer becomes a four-headed arrow) and drag to desired location.

12 Click the following WordArt and Drawing toolbar buttons to apply special effects:

- **Format** button to open the Format dialog box, to add more than one fill color.

- **Character Spacing** button to make the characters closer or further apart.

- **Rotate** button to rotate the text in any desired orientation.

- **Fill Color** drop-down button to change the interior color of the drawing.

- **Line Color** drop-down button to change the color of the outline.

- **Font Color** drop-down button to change the color of interior text.

- **Shadow** drop-down to choose a shadow.

- **3-D** drop-down to choose a three dimensional effect.

Advanced Tools

Word has many sophisticated features that are used for specialized purposes. This section will cover the creation of indexes and tables of contents, the use of passwords to protect your documents, and the creation and use of styles. You will also learn to produce macros, which provide you with shortcuts for accessing commonly performed tasks. Word can also help you to create forms and letters, and to merge information from different sources.

Document Map

Use the document map feature to navigate documents that contain headings that have been formatted with Styles or Outlines.

Notes:

- To see more detail, click the minus sign next to a document heading to display subordinate headings.

- Use the IntelliMouse wheel to display subordinate headings by holding shift and rotating the wheel.

1 Click **View**, **Document Map** to open the Document Map pane.

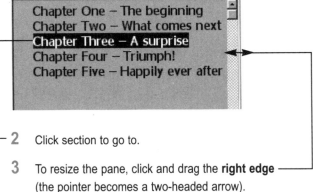

2 Click section to go to.

3 To resize the pane, click and drag the **right edge** (the pointer becomes a two-headed arrow).

4 To close the pane, click **View**, **Document Map**.

174

Continue

Embed Objects

The Embed feature is used to add information from a file created in another program to a Word file.

Notes:

- The embedded information becomes part of the Word (destination) file, but the source program can be launched from the embedded information.

1 In the source file, copy the desired information to the clipboard.

2 In the Word destination file, click **Edit**, **Paste Special**. The Paste Special dialog box opens.

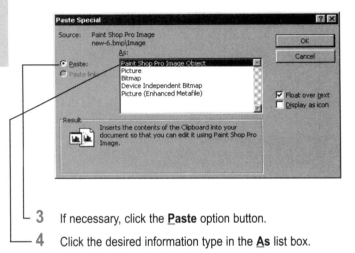

3 If necessary, click the **Paste** option button.

4 Click the desired information type in the **As** list box.

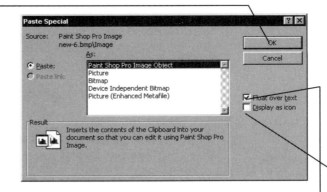

5   Click the **Float over text** checkbox to position the object
       independent of the text surrounding it.
       OR
       Clear the **Float over text** checkbox to anchor the object
       to the current insertion point position.

6   Click the **Display as icon** to convert the embedded
       information to an icon representing the source program.

7   Click **OK**.

Edit an Embedded Object

Double-click the object to launch the source program.

Forms

Word includes many tools to create on-screen or printed forms that include drop-down boxes, check boxes and other advanced features.

1   Right-click on any toolbar and click Forms to display the Forms toolbar.

2   Design your document as desired.

3   To insert a field, click the tool button, then click the document where desired:

   - **Text** field button ![abl] to insert a field that can hold a varying amount of text

   - **Check Box** field button ![✓] to insert a yes/no field

   - **Drop-down** from field button ![] to insert a field with multiple choices

4   Double-click a field to customize it.

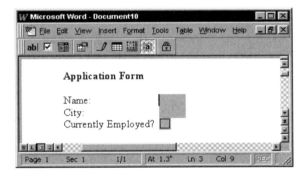

5   If desired, click the **Draw Table** button ![✏] to insert a custom table.

178

6 Click the **Insert Table** button 🖾 to insert a custom table.

7 Click the **Insert Frame** button 🖾 to insert a frame.

8 Click the Form Field Shading button 🖾 to make fields more or less prominent.

9 When finished, click the Protect Form button 🖾.

10 If the form is to be used as an on-screen form, save it as a template: click the Save button 🖾 and in the Save As dialog, in the Save as Type text box, select Template. (See **Templates**).

Use an On-Screen Form

1 Open a document based on the form template (See New Document).

2 Click **Tab** to go to the next field.

3 Click **Shift + Tab** to go to the previous field.

Indexes: Mark Index Entries

Word can automatically create an index based on words you select, or based on
a concordance file.

Using the Dialog Box

1   Select text to use as an index entry, or click the location
    to which you want an index entry to refer.

2   Press **Alt + Shift + X** to open the Mark Index Entry
    dialog box.

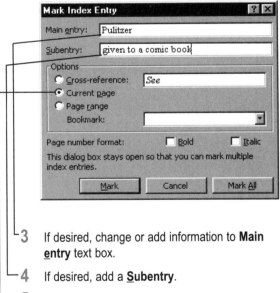

3   If desired, change or add information to **Main
    entry** text box.

4   If desired, add a **Subentry**.

5   Click index option desired:
    - **Cross-reference** to refer to another index entry,
      then type the entry in the following text box.
    - **Current page** to refer to current page only.
    - **Page range** to list a range defined by a bookmark
      (see **Bookmark**), type or choose the bookmark name.

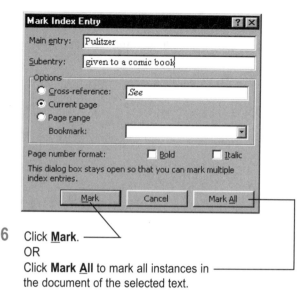

6 Click **Mark**.
OR
Click **Mark All** to mark all instances in the document of the selected text.

Notes:

- A concordance file is an index file that contains two columns: one that contains a list of the items you wish to index, and the second that contains a list of the entries to generate from the text in the first column.

Create a Concordance File

1 Create a new file.

2 Create a table with two columns (see **Table**).

3 Type the text to search for in the first column.

4 Type the text to use in the index entry in the second column.

5 Save the file.

6 Open the main document file.

7 Click **Insert**, **Index and Table** to open the Index and Tables dialog box.

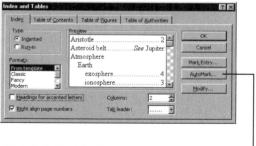

8 Click **AutoMark** button

9 Select the concordance file you created.

10 Click **Open**.

Indexes: Create a Final Index

After the Index has been built, you must create the final output of the Index.

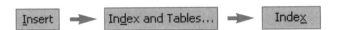

Notes:

- Use a concordance file to create a list of words or phrases to index throughout a document and to automatically mark the items where ever they occur (see **previous page**).

Create an Index

1 Click where you want the index to begin.

2 Click **Insert**, **Index and Tables** to open the Index and Tables dialog box.

3 Click the **Index** tab to bring it to the front.

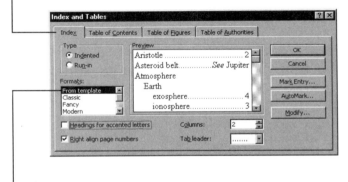

4 Click desired style in the **Formats** list box (a preview appears to the right).

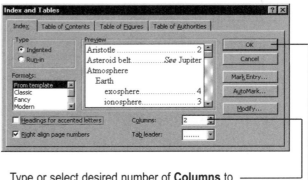

5 Type or select desired number of **Columns** to use on the page.

6 Click **OK**.

Link Objects

The Link feature is used to add information from a file created in another program to a Word file.

Edit ➤ Paste Special... ➤ ⊙ Paste link:

Notes:

- The linked information remains part of the source file, so when the source file is changed, the information in the Word file (the destination file) is automatically updated.

1 In the source file, copy the desired information to the clipboard.

2 In the Word destination file, click **Edit**, **Paste Special**. The Paste Special dialog box opens.

3 Click the **Paste link** option button.

4 Click the desired information type in the **As** list box.

5 Click the **Float over text** checkbox to position the object independent of the text surrounding it.
OR
Clear the **Float over text** checkbox to anchor the object to the current insertion point position.

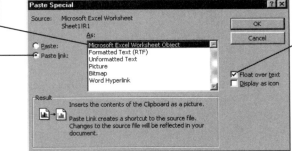

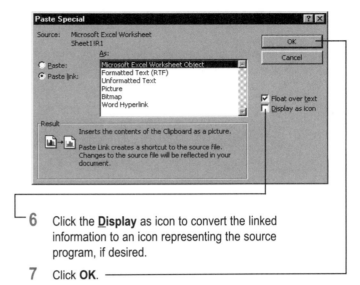

6   Click the **Display** as icon to convert the linked information to an icon representing the source program, if desired.

7   Click **OK**.

Edit a Linked Object

Double-click the object to open the source file.

Macros

A Macro is a recording of text and commands that can then be played back.
Use macros to automate repetitive tasks.

Tools ➤ Macro ➤ ● Record New Macro...

Notes:

- It's handy to create a macro that opens your favorite template and assign the macro to a toolbar button.

- If, while you're recording a macro, you need to perform actions you don't want to record, click the Pause button. Click Pause again to restart recording.

- Do not use spaces in the Macro name. Word will not be able to recognize them.

Record Macro

1   Click **Tools**, **Macro**, **Record New Macro** to open the Record Macro dialog box.

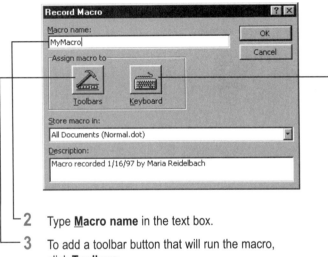

2   Type **Macro name** in the text box.

3   To add a toolbar button that will run the macro, click **Toolbars**.

4   In the **Commands** list box that appears, click and drag the new macro name to the desired spot on the toolbar.

5   To assign a keyboard shortcut that will run the macro, click **Keyboard**.

6   Type key combination (usually using the Ctrl or Alt keys in combination with letters or numbers) in the **Press new shortcut** key text box. If the key combination you type is currently used by another command, that command will appear below.

7   Click **Assign** when finished.

8 Click **Close** to return to the document window.
   The macro toolbar is displayed.

9 Perform the actions that you wish to record.

10 When finished, click the Stop Recording button ![stop button] on the Macro toolbar.

Play Macro

If you assigned your macro to a toolbar button or a shortcut key sequence, it can be played back by accessing that button or key combination. It may also be played back by doing the following:

1 Click **Tools**, **Macro**, **Macros** to open the Macro dialog box.

2 In the list box, click desired **Macro name** to play.

3 Click **Run**.

Mail Merge

The Merge feature combines text from one document with text from another in a systematic way.

Tools ➡ Mail Merge...

Notes:

- A list of names and addresses may be combined with a form letter to create personalized letters.

1   Create a new document or open a document to use as your main document.

2   Click **Tools**, **Mail Merge** to open the Mail Merge dialog box.

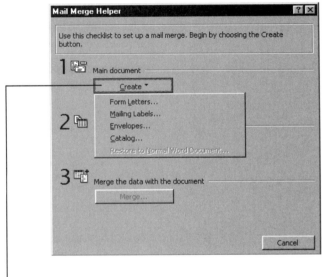

3   Click **Create** button and click desired type of **Main document**.

4 Click the **Active** window button.

5 Click the **Get Data** button to choose a data source for your merge:
  • **Create Data Source** to type a list to use
  • **Open Data Source** to choose a Word, Access or other file containing the list to use.
  • **Use Address Book** to use the Microsoft address book list.

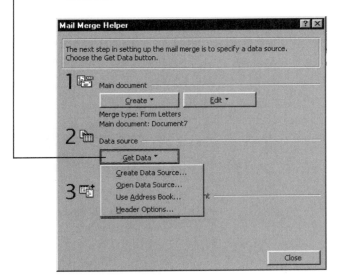

Mail Merge Helper ? ▣

The next step in setting up the mail merge is to specify a data source. Choose the Get Data button.

1 ▣ Main document
  Create ▾ | Edit ▾
  Merge type: Form Letters
  Main document: Document7

2 ▣ Data source
  Get Data ▾
    Create Data Source...
    Open Data Source...
    Use Address Book...
    Header Options...

3 ▣

Close

6 Follow instructions on screen to use your chosen data source.

7 If necessary, click the **Edit** button to return to the main document.

8 Compose and format main document: point and click where you want to add the first field to contain changing information from your data source.

9 On the merge toolbar, click the Insert Merge Field ▼ button and click desired field name.

10 Continue composing main document, adding merge fields where desired.

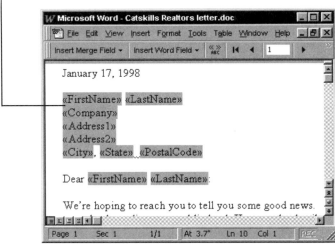

11 To see the main document as it will appear with data, click the View Merged Data button ⟪⟫

12 Save and name the main document.

13 To merge the main document and the data source, click desired button:

- Click Merge to New Document button ▣ to create a new document containing copies of the main document merged with the data source list.

- Click Merge to Printer button ▣ to print the merged copies of main document.

Password

Keep others from opening your file with a secret password. Make sure you remember the password: without it, you can't open the file!

Notes:

- You can also protect a document from being changed by others by saving the document as a **Read-only** file. Click File, Save as, click the Option button and select the Read Only Recommended option. See also **Protect Documents**.

1 Click **File**, **Save As** to open the Save As dialog box.

2 Click the **Options** button to open the options dialog box.

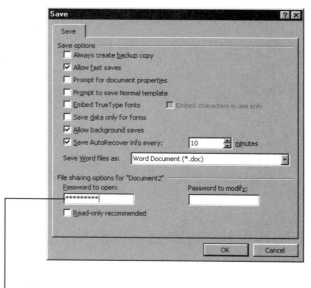

3 In **Password to open** text box, type desired password. (Your password will be indicated with asterisks.)

4 In **Password to modify** text box, type desired password.

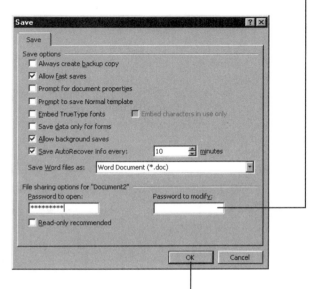

5 Click **OK**.

6 Confirm your password by retyping it.

7 Click **OK**.

8 Save and name the document as desired.

Protect Documents

Keeps documents from being inadvertently or intentionally changed. An entire document, or specified section can be protected

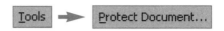

Notes:

- To password protect a document from being opened, see **Password Protect**.

1 Click **Tools**, **Protect Document** to open the Protect Document dialog box.

2 Click option button for protection desired:
- **Tracked changes** to format any editing as a tracked change (see **Track Changes**)
- **Comments** to allow the addition of comments only (see **Comments**)
- **Forms** to protect only specific document sections. Click the **Sections** button to specify.

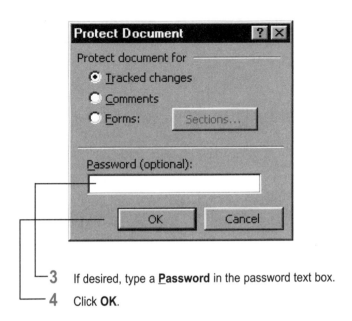

3 If desired, type a **Password** in the password text box.

4 Click **OK**.

Remove Protection

Click **Tools**, **Unprotect document**.

Styles: Apply a Style

Styles are used to save or apply a set of character and paragraph formats to selected text.

Notes:

Notes:

- Word comes with a number of pre-formatted styles. You may create and save your own.

- If you use styles in a document and later decide to modify them, the text that was formatted with the style will also change.

Toolbar

1   Click and drag over text to select it.
    OR
    Point to and click where you intend to type new text.

2   Click the Style drop-down button  and choose desired style to apply.

Dialog Box

Format → Style...

1   Click and drag over text to select it.
    OR
    Point and click where you intend to type new text.

2 Click **Format**, **Style** to open the Styles dialog box.

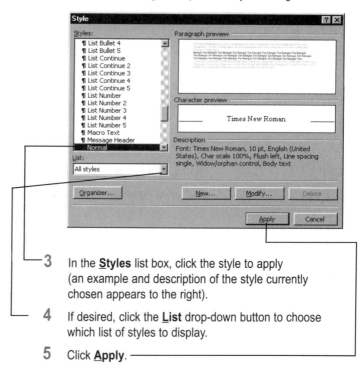

3 In the **Styles** list box, click the style to apply (an example and description of the style currently chosen appears to the right).

4 If desired, click the **List** drop-down button to choose which list of styles to display.

5 Click **Apply**.

Styles: Create and Modify a Style

Create a new style for any set of character or paragraph formatting codes that you expect to use again in another location.

1 Click **Format**, **Style** to open the Styles dialog box.

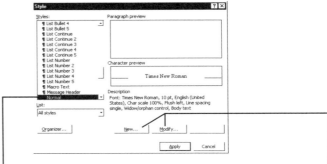

2 In the **Styles** list box, click the style to modify (an example and description of the style currently chosen appears to the right. (If desired, click the **List** drop-down button to choose which list of styles to display.)

3 Click **Modify** to open the Modify Style dialog box.
OR
Click **New** to open the New Style dialog box.

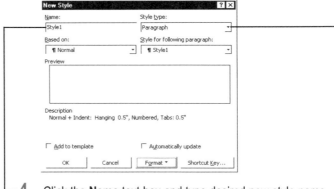

4 Click the **Name** text box and type desired new style name.

5 Click the **Style type** drop-down button and choose:
- **Paragraph** to specify both character and paragraph formatting
- **Character** to specify only character formatting

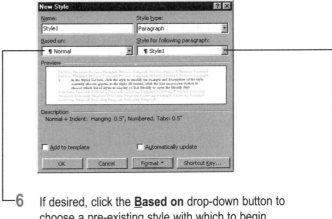

6 If desired, click the **Based on** drop-down button to choose a pre-existing style with which to begin.

7 Current formatting appears in the **Preview box** and is described beneath.

8 Click **Format** to choose characteristics to change.

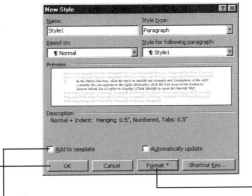

9 Change text formatting as desired.

10 Click the **Add to template** check box to add the style to future documents created with the same template.

11 Click **OK** when you are finished.

12 In the Style dialog box, click **Apply** to apply the new style OR

click **Cancel** to return to the document.

Style Gallery

Use the Style Gallery feature to view examples of style templates and to see a preview of the effect a different style would have on the current document or a sample document.

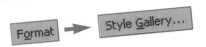

Notes:

- To see a list of all the formatting styles used in a particular template, click the Style samples Preview option.

1   Click **Format**, **Style Gallery** to open the Style Gallery dialog box.

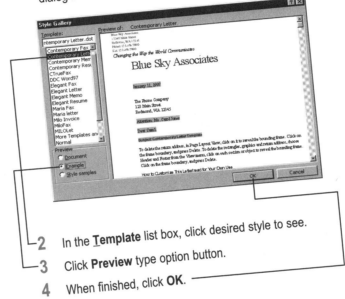

2   In the **Template** list box, click desired style to see.

3   Click **Preview** type option button.

4   When finished, click **OK**.

200

Continue

→

Table of Contents

With advance preparation of the document, the Table of Contents feature automatically creates tables of contents of a variety of styles and levels.

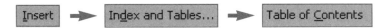

Insert ➡ Index and Tables... ➡ Table of Contents

Notes:

- If you see a field code where your table of contents should be, click it and press Alt + F9.

1. In the document on which the table of contents is to be based, format the entries in either of the following ways:
   - Using **Styles**, apply heading styles one through nine to headings you wish to include (see **Styles**).
   - Using **Outline** view, apply levels one through nine to headings you wish to include (see **Outline**).

2. Click document where you want to insert the table of contents.

3. Click **Insert**, **Index and Tables** to open the **Index and Tables** dialog box.

4. Click the **Table of Contents** tab to bring it to the front.

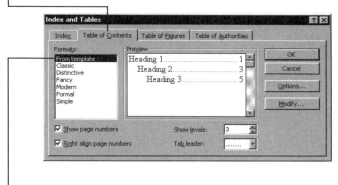

5. In the **Formats** list box, click desired style (see a preview at the right).

202

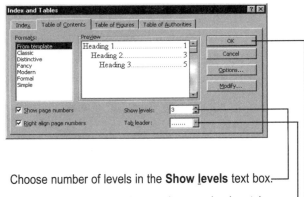

6 Choose number of levels in the **Show levels** text box.

7 Click the **Tab leader** list box to choose a leader style.

8 When finished, click **OK**.

Update a Table of Contents

Update your table of contents when the contents of your document change.

1 Click anywhere in the table of contents.

2 Press **F9**.

Index

Notes

Notes

Short Course Learning Books
Approximately 25 hours of instruction per book

We sliced our learning books into short courses, *introductory* & *intermediate*.

- We extracted pages from our Fast-teach Learning books and created shortened versions.
- Each book comes with a data disk to eliminate typing the exercise.

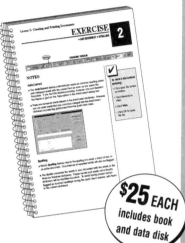

$25 EACH includes book and data disk

Title	Cat. No.	Title	Cat. No.	Title	Cat. No.
Access 2 Introductory	AB-10	Microsoft Office 4.3 Introductory	AB-14	WordPerfect 6.1 Win Introductory	AB-1
Access 7 Introductory	AB-23	Microsoft Office Win 95 Introductory	AB-15	WordPerfect 6.1 Win Intermediate	AB-2
DOS Introductory	AB-13	PowerPoint 4 Introductory	AB-11	Word 6 Windows Introductory	AB-4
Excel 5 Windows Introductory	AB-7	PowerPoint 7 Introductory	AB-24	Word 6 Windows Intermediate	AB-5
Excel 5 Windows Intermediate	AB-8	Windows 3.1 Introductory	AB-12	Word 7 Windows 95 Introductory	AB-17
Excel 7 Windows 95 Introductory	AB-20				

New Short Courses (College Level).... **$25**ea.	
Teacher Manual and Exercise Solutions on Diskette .... **$12**ea.	
Files saved in Word 7	
Title	**Cat No.**
Microsoft Office Windows 95	AB-15
Pagemaker 6 Intro	AB-16
No Teacher Manual	
Word 7 Intro	AB-17
Word 7 Intermediate	AB-18
Word 7 Advanced	AB-19
Excel 7 Intro	AB-20
Excel 7 Intermediate	AB-21
PowerPoint 7 Intro	AB-15
Access 7 Intro	AB-23

DDC Publishing 275 Madison Avenue, New York, NY 10016

- - - - - - - - - ORDER FORM - - - - - - - - - -

QTY.	CAT. NO.	DESCRIPTION

Check enclosed. Add $2.50 for postage & handling & $1 postage for each additional guide. NY State residents add local sales tax.

Visa ☐   Mastercard ☐   **100% Refund Guarantee**

No._____ Exp._____

Name_____

Firm _____

Address_____

City, State, Zip _____

Phone (800) 528-3897   Fax (800) 528-3862

(DDC) Quick Reference Guides
find software answers faster
because you read less

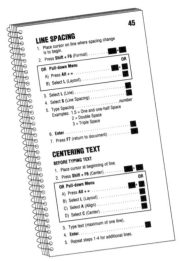

FREE TEMPLATE ON BACK COVER

What took you five minutes now takes one minute.

The illustrated instructions put your fingers on the correct keys – fast. We tell you what to do in five or six words. Sometimes only two.

No narration or exposition. Just "press this – type that" illustrated commands.

Spiral binding keeps pages flat so you can type what you read.

The time you save will pay for the book the first day. Free template on back cover.

Office Managers

Look at the production time you can gain when these quick-find, low-cost guides go to work for you. It will pay for the guides the first day you use them.

(DDC) *Computer based training puts an interactive teacher in your computer*

For Microsoft® Office Windows® 95 to teach Word 7, Excel 7, Access 7, and PowerPoint 7

You hear, you see, you do, you learn.

Our teachers present instructions to you orally and visually live and on screen. Our Multimedia CD ROM takes the written word off the page, explains the concept, and tells you what to do. This teacher sits at your elbow, sight unseen, ready to correct your errors and tell you how to do it, until you get it correct.

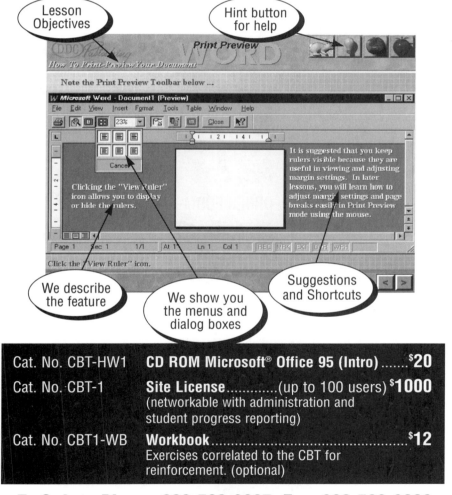

Cat. No. CBT-HW1	**CD ROM Microsoft® Office 95 (Intro)** $20
Cat. No. CBT-1	**Site License** ....(up to 100 users) $1000
	(networkable with administration and student progress reporting)
Cat. No. CBT1-WB	**Workbook** $12
	Exercises correlated to the CBT for reinforcement. (optional)

To Order - Phone: 800-528-3897   Fax: 800-528-3862

More Fast-teach Learning Books

Did we make one for you?

Title	Cat. No.
Corel WordPerfect 7 for Win 95	Z12
DOS 5–6.2 (Book & Disk)	D9
DOS + Windows	Z7
Excel 5 for Windows	E9
Excel 7 for Windows 95	XL7
INTERNET	Z15
Lotus 1-2-3 Rel. 2.2–4.0 for DOS	L9
Lotus 1-2-3 Rel. 4 & 5 for Windows	B9
Microsoft Office	M9
Microsoft Office for Windows 95	Z6
Windows 3.1 – A Quick Study	WQS-1
Windows 95	Z3
Word 2 for Windows	K9
Word 6 for Windows	1-WDW6
Word 7 for Windows 95	Z10
WordPerfect 5.0 & 5.1 for DOS	W9
WordPerfect 6 for DOS	P9
WordPerfect 6 for Windows	Z9
WordPerfect 6.1 for Windows	H9
Works 3 for Windows	1-WKW3
Works 4 for Windows 95	Z8

DESKTOP PUBLISHING LEARNING BOOKS	
Word 6 for Windows	Z2
WordPerfect 5.1 for DOS	WDB
WordPerfect 6 for Windows	F9
WordPerfect 6.1 for Windows	Z5

Learning **The Internet**

What we teach:

- Searching Techniques

- Browsers/Search Engines
  -MS Explorer
  -Netscape
  -Yahoo
  -Web Crawler

- Sources of Information
  -Telnet
  -Usenet
  -E-mail
  -WWW Virtual Library
  -Electronic Encyclopedias
  -CD-ROM

- Using the Information

  -Notepad

  -Word Processors

  -Compiling

  -Download Utilities

Cat. No. Z-15   ISBN 1-56243-345-8

Learning the Internet......$27

Learning the Internet Simulation CD-ROM

- Now you don't need to connect to the Web to teach Internet concepts.

- Simulates the sites and hyperlinks used in DDC's *Learning the Internet* book.

Cat. No. Z-15CD..........$20

275 Madison Avenue,
New York, NY 10016